OLDER AND WISER

Lawrence Thompson

Older and Wiser:
The Economics of Public Pensions

THE URBAN INSTITUTE PRESS
Washington, D.C.

THE URBAN INSTITUTE PRESS
2100 M Street, N.W.
Washington, D.C. 20037

Editorial Advisory Board

William Gorham   Demetra S. Nightingale
Craig G. Coelen   Marilyn Moon
Kathleen Courrier   George E. Peterson
Adele V. Harrell   Felicity Skidmore

Copyright © 1998. The Urban Institute. All rights reserved. Except for short quotes, no part of this book may be reproduced or utilized in any form or by any means, electronic or mechanical, including photocopying, recording, or by information storage or retrieval system, without written permission from The Urban Institute Press.

Library of Congress Cataloging-in-Publication Data

Thompson, Lawrence H., 1943–

Older and Wiser: The Economics of Public Pensions/
Lawrence H. Thompson.

Includes index.

1. Social security. 2. Social security—Finance. 3. Social security—OECD countries. 4. Social security—IECD countries—Finance. I. Title.

HD7091.T514   1998   98-10300
368.4—DC21   CIP

ISBN 0-87766-679-2 (paper, alk. paper)
ISBN 0-87766-678-4 (cloth, alk. paper)

Printed in the United States of America.

Distributed in North America by
University Press of America
4720 Boston Way
Lanham, MD 20706

BOARD OF TRUSTEES
Richard B. Fisher
 Chairman
Katharine Graham
 Vice Chairman
Joel L. Fleishman
 Vice Chairman
William Gorham
 President
Joan Toland Bok
Marcia L. Carsey
Carol Thompson Cole
Richard C. Green, Jr.
Jack Kemp
Robert S. McNamara
Charles L. Mee, Jr.
Robert C. Miller
Lucio Noto
Hugh B. Price
Sol Price
Robert M. Solow
Dick Thornburgh
Judy Woodruff

LIFE TRUSTEES
Warren E. Buffett
James E. Burke
Joseph A. Califano, Jr.
William T. Coleman, Jr.
John M. Deutch
Anthony Downs
Eugene G. Fubini
George J.W. Goodman
Fernando A. Guerra, M.D.
Aileen C. Hernandez
Carla A. Hills
Vernon E. Jordan, Jr.
Edward H. Levi
Bayless A. Manning
Stanley Marcus
David O. Maxwell
Arjay Miller
J. Irwin Miller
Lois D. Rice
Elliot L. Richardson
William D. Ruckelshaus
Herbert E. Scarf
Charles L. Schultze
William W. Scranton
Cyrus R. Vance
James Vorenberg
Mortimer B. Zuckerman

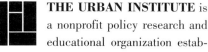

THE URBAN INSTITUTE is a nonprofit policy research and educational organization established in Washington, D.C., in 1968. Its staff investigates the social and economic problems confronting the nation and public and private means to alleviate them. The Institute disseminates significant findings of its research through the publications program of its Press. The goals of the Institute are to sharpen thinking about societal problems and efforts to solve them, improve government decisions and performance, and increase citizen awareness of important policy choices.

Through work that ranges from broad conceptual studies to administrative and technical assistance, Institute researchers contribute to the stock of knowledge available to guide decisionmaking in the public interest.

Conclusions or opinions expressed in Institute publications are those of the authors and do not necessarily reflect the views of staff members, officers or trustees of the Institute, advisory groups, or any organizations that provide financial support to the Institute.

Acknowledgments

The material in this book was developed as part of a larger effort entitled "The Stockholm Initiative," which is sponsored by the International Social Security Association (ISSA). The initiative was launched under the leadership of K. G. Scherman and is described in his Introduction to this book. The book benefited from much interaction with members of the Geneva-based Secretariat of the ISSA, particularly Dalmer D. Hoskins, Secretary General, and Warren McGillivray, Chief of the Studies and Operations Branch.

The ISSA Secretariat formed a technical panel which met in Berlin on 28–29 April, 1997, to review earlier drafts and offer comments, criticisms, and suggestions. I wish to express my appreciation to the members of that panel who were willing to give generously of their time in order to improve this product. The panel chair was Professor Winfried Schmähl, University of Bremen, Germany. Panel members included: Christopher Daykin, United Kingdom Government Actuary; Professor Bert de Vries, Erasmus University, Rotterdam; Catherine Drummond, Director of General Programs, Human Resources Development, Canada; Professor Tor Eriksen, University of Gotheburg, Sweden; Professor Neil Gilbert, University of California, Berkeley; Colin Gillion, Director, Social Security Department, International Labour Office, Geneva; Peter Hicks, Consultant, Social Policy Division, OECD, Paris; Robert Hagemann, Prinicipal Economist, International Monetary Fund Office in Europe, Paris; Robert Holzmann, Director of Social Protection, The World Bank, Washington; Esko Kalimo, Director, Research and Development Centre,

Social Insurance Institution, Finland; Klaus Michaelis, Member of the Directorate, Federal Insurance Institute for Salaried Employees, Germany; Emmanuel Reynaud, Institute for Economic and Social Research, Paris; Stanford Ross, Former Public Trustee of Social Security and Medicare, United States; Fumio Sasaki, Commissioner of the Social Insurance Agency, Japan; Giovanni Tamburi, Watson Wyatt Limited, Geneva; Horacio Templo, Chief Actuary of the Social Security System, Philippines; and Safwan Toqan, Director General of the Social Security Corporation, Jordan. Valuable additional suggestions on earlier drafts came from Professors Joseph F. Quinn, Boston College; Peter Diamond, Massachusetts Institute of Technology; and Alan L. Gustman of Dartmouth College. I gave careful consideration to all of the suggestions and made many changes as a result. I accept sole responsibility, however, for the tone and contents of these papers.

Computational and research assistance was provided by my associate at the Urban Institute, Adam Carasso.

Financial and in-kind support for this publication have been received from ISSA member institutions in Austria, Canada, Finland, Germany, Italy, Japan, Mauritius, the Netherlands, Norway, the Philippines, and Sweden.

Contents

	Acknowledgments	vii
	Foreword	xi
	Introduction *by Karl Gustaf Scherman* *President of the International Social Security Association*	xiii
1	Overview and Summary	1
2	Reasons for Creating Mandatory Retirement Programs	25
3	The Economic Cost of Supporting the Retired	37
4	The Effect of Pensions on Saving and Investment	51
5	The Effect of Pensions on Labor Supply	71
6	Public Pensions and International Competitiveness	85
7	The Mathematics of Pension Contribution Rates	97
8	Choices of Pension Approaches and Transitions Between Approaches	115
9	Risks of Mid-Career Economic and Demographic Changes	133
10	Ensuring Income Adequacy Throughout Retirement	151
	Index	169
	About the Author	177

Foreword

Pay-as-you-go public pension programs are the backbone of retirement security in most industrialized countries. For the first half-century following their introduction in the major democracies, they enjoyed great favor not only as social but also as economic institutions. During the past decade and a half they have been criticized increasingly sharply, however, as countries the world over debate ways to improve macroeconomic performance, respond to changing population characteristics, and reflect shifting values as to the role of individual versus collective provision for old age.

The sharpest critiques of traditional public pension schemes come from an economic perspective—with attacks on their overall economic effects as well as their fiscal dynamics and adequacy as sources of retirement income. This book addresses each of these issues in turn. One of its major contributions is to throw new light on how economic growth affects the costs of supporting the elderly. Many advocate increasing economic growth at least in part as a way to reduce the costs of supporting future retirees. As this book makes clear, increasing economic growth could have the reverse effect. By raising living standards among the working population, it could create an incentive to retire at younger ages. It could also reduce resistance among the working generation to rising contribution rates. In both cases, faster growth would in fact increase the cost of supporting future generations of retirees.

The Urban Institute has been a major contributor to the debate about public pensions in the U.S. policy context, with *Retooling Social Security for the 21st Century: Right and Wrong Approaches to Reform* by C. Eugene Steuerle and Jon M. Bakija and *Entitlements and the Elderly: Protecting Promises, Recognizing Realities* by Marilyn Moon and Janemarie Mulvey being two recent examples. This book, which is also the first step in the International

Social Security Association's search for a new consensus on public pension design and coverage, broadens the context of the discussion.

One of the Institute's important goals is to anticipate important problems early enough to stimulate reasoned, informed debate on alternative policy solutions before a crisis hits. It is my hope that this timely book will help widen understanding of the economic issues underlying the public pension debate among policymakers and the publics they serve.

William Gorham
President

Introduction

The Social Insurance Reform Debate: In Search of a New Consensus

K.G. Scherman
President of the International Social Security Association

Public social protection for those not able to support themselves is crucial to the well-being of individuals and families, and to the functioning of the economy and society as a whole. In addition to the dignity and independence social security protection affords beneficiaries, cash benefits are important in sustaining consumer demand. A well-designed social security system directly improves the functioning of the labor market. And proper health care for all is important for the development of the economy. In sum, social security constitutes an effective program for fostering social peace and economic cohesion in modern societies.

Now, however, social security is alleged to be a major cause of the current unsatisfactory economic performance in many industrialized countries. To name but one of the critics, the World Bank, in its 1994 report, *Averting the Old Age Crisis*, criticized publicly managed pay-as-you-go defined benefit schemes for high and rising payroll tax rates, misallocation of public resources, lost opportunity to increase long-term saving, failure to redistribute to low-income groups, growth of a large hidden implicit public pension debt, and fiscal unsustainability.

The questioning of the role and function of social security is directly linked to the more general reevaluation of the roles of the state and the public sector in society in a period of severe economic and financial constraints. Many parts of the world are currently experiencing serious economic conditions. In much of Western Europe, for example, unemployment remains well above 10 percent and social welfare charges are over 20 percent. In Eastern and Central Europe, Africa, Asia, and the Caribbean, unemployment reaches upwards of 30 percent.

The current debate, together with the economic constraints, already has led to significant reductions in the level of social protection in many countries. At the same time, due to accelerated social change, new risks are emerging and some previous risks are growing in importance. The number of people living in "risk-prone" environments is increasing.

Many countries have attempted to deal with rising health costs through higher cost sharing and more restrictive eligibility conditions. Rising levels of unemployment and the increasing use of casual and part-time workers have reduced access to sickness insurance and other social benefits. Unemployed younger persons may not yet be participating in social security programs and, in both industrialized and developing countries, a growing informal labor market may permanently separate many from the social protection system.

New risks are emerging in the economic transitions now occurring in Central and Eastern Europe, where centrally planned economies are being replaced with more market-oriented economies, and in many developing countries, where reforms are being introduced to eliminate glaring inefficiencies. While structural reforms are needed in order to deal with long-standing problems, the transitions often involve hardships and dislocations. Living conditions for people affected by these transitions have deteriorated, and the social arrangements that should serve as a cushion are often inadequate.

Meanwhile, increased longevity in both industrialized and developing countries has introduced new challenges. One challenge is the need to provide care for the growing numbers of elderly who wish to remain in their homes and communities. Can social security systems be restructured to recognize a more equitable sharing of family responsibilities between men and women for both child care and elder care? Another challenge is the growing number of persons who leave the labor force before the eligibility age fixed in the old-age pension system. Many countries would like to raise their pension ages to alleviate the financing problems generated by longer lifespans. Introducing such changes in the face of declining employment rates among older workers, however, threatens to create a new class of vulnerable elderly either with no steady source of income until they reach the higher retirement age or condemned to live the rest of their lives on permanently reduced pensions.

Whatever one's opinion about the many issues involved and the merits of various points of view in the debate, it is obvious that a new environment creates new challenges. The discussion of how social security for a new age can best be designed and implemented must take a broad spectrum of options into account: the family, voluntary arrangements of different kinds, private insurance, social assistance, mandatory savings plans, and social insurance. Some of these options are alternatives, and many of them can be combined into a set of measures that together offer individuals the security they need. But how the pieces are put together in individual countries—how the social welfare system is restructured—is fundamentally a political process.

Are our national political systems capable of reshaping the welfare system? We do not yet know. Modern social institutions have developed mainly during periods of almost continuous high levels of economic growth. As a consequence, decisions were taken in trust that tomorrow's resources would always be larger than those of today. Now we realize that this will not always be the case. But we have yet to find out whether these democratic systems have the capacity to build new models that are less sensitive to fluctuations in economic growth.

How do people truly want their society organized? This is the fundamental question. Inherent and acquired cultural values have a great impact on how people form their opinions. Throughout the world there is a broad underlying consensus that the state has a responsibility to arrange at least some basic support for those who cannot support themselves and who are not cared for in any other way. Given this common underlying basic value as a starting point, it is possible that state intervention in the social welfare field and the ensuing public debate can influence the evolution of a consensus. It remains to be explored how far and how deeply such a process can reach.

The expansion of the public welfare order in many countries, which has been very rapid and dramatic indeed, has been based largely on how politicians have interpreted the public debate. The public support for the expansion might very well have been exaggerated in this process. If so, the support might collapse in times of financial constrains for the ordinary citizen, who has to come up with the contributions needed to sustain the system.

A well-functioning social security system is a basic element in any modern society. Very few issues are as politically and economically important as the ongoing reform in the welfare area. A country which does not make sure that its welfare system enjoys widespread confidence among the population should not expect the population to have confidence in the future. Thus, reforms which strengthen people's confidence in the systems will also strengthen the economy.

What is dramatic is that the same questions are being asked everywhere: What is happening in the national economy? What is the relationship between the economy and social protection measures? Can we afford social welfare protection? The fact that these questions are the same despite countries' widely differing social and economic systems leads to an inescapable conclusion: Current economic theories are not in harmony with current ambitions in the social arena. We need to better understand the factors that cause certain models to function more effectively in some countries than in others. Such understanding is crucial to building a new consensus on the range of acceptable approaches for balancing economic and social policy needs. Taking into account the great diversity among countries, including their different experiences, traditions, and institutions, this new consensus must encompass different national approaches.

Representatives of several member institutions of the International Social Security Association (ISSA) have requested its assistance in understanding and helping to participate in the debate. At a meeting in Stockholm, the ISSA Bureau authorized the Association's President to explore more fully the role that the ISSA might play. As a result, the ISSA launched the Stockholm Initiative, *The Social Security Reform Debate: In Search of a New Consensus*. The overall objective of the Initiative is to promote a dialogue on the most important social protection issues and facilitate a new consensus on acceptable approaches to social security. This project will assist policymakers and social security organizations throughout the world to understand the various arguments and choose reform alternatives that best suit their circumstances.

Many international agencies and organizations are now engaged in trying to broaden the debate in order to cope with the tremendous task of reforming social security systems. All realize that public confidence in the reform process and a reconciliation of economic and social policy are key elements. If a new consensus is to be forged, it is essential that economists and representatives from the social welfare policy arena discuss, listen to one another, and exchange ideas and opinions. I am convinced such a consensus can be achieved, and that this first volume will contribute to it. By opening our minds to one another's views, listening, and cooperating, we can contribute to a better future for humanity.

This volume covers critical issues in the current debate on economic and financial aspects of pensions, as well as vital issues about the social consequences of various approaches. It meets pressing needs for clarification of various aspects of the intense debate now going on in various parts of the world.

The aim of the Stockholm Initiative is to expand the debate to all components of social security as well as to the relationship between social security and the functioning of society as a whole. The interdependence of social and economic circumstances in a country and the influence of national culture, values, and traditions on how social security arrangements function must be investigated. These are complicated matters indeed and the way in which they should be addressed requires careful analysis and a broad consultative process.

All components of social security must be studied. In addition to pensions, health care and unemployment insurance are especially important branches of social security and will be covered in the Stockholm Initiative's next step. Each of these branches has quite different conditions and problems. But when it comes to broader considerations about how social security functions in society they have much in common. Topics that cover more than a single branch include the creation and maintenance of public trust in government and social security, social security as a factor of production, the impact of economic globalization on social security, and changes in the organization of social security institutions resulting from changes in society.

Yet another approach would be to study the role of social security in different societies by investigating such issues as recognition of the need for reform, and how the reform process can ensure that concerns about adequacy, financial sustainability, political feasibility, economic coherence, and public support are properly taken into account.

Whatever the approach, the fundamental challenge for further studies is clear. We must be able to answer the following questions: *What are the preconditions for social security in a modern society? What are their implications? How can reforms be implemented effectively, and what are the criteria for success? How can these issues be studied so as to best serve as a basis for the reform process?*

On behalf of the International Social Security Association, I invite all of you to join the investigation.

Chapter One

Overview and Summary

During the past fifteen years, debate about and actual change in the scope and structure of national pension systems have grown to unprecedented levels. This intense focus on pension systems and institutions is occurring throughout the world, in fully developed and developing economies alike. It is being driven by a number of factors that vary in mix from one part of the globe to another. These include the need or desire to restructure entire economic systems, reinvigorate ineffective pension institutions, or improve social protection in concert with improving economic conditions. Debate is often occasioned by the hope that alternative pension structures will improve macroeconomic performance and help respond to changing demographics, or the desire to reflect changes in social philosophy about the relative importance of individual and collective provision for retirement.

One of the most prominent features of the current debate is sharp criticism of the pay-as-you-go, public pension programs that are the primary means of providing retirement income in many industrialized countries. For decades, these programs were widely viewed as valuable social and economic institutions. Today, they are often accused of costing too much, reflecting outmoded social philosophies, and having undesirable consequences for the economy. The previous consensus in support of these pay-as-you-go, public programs has broken down.

In the face of an increasingly polarized debate, the member organizations of the International Social Security Association (ISSA) asked the Association to help lead the search for a new consensus. The logical way to begin this search is with a careful review of the various arguments put forward by both critics and defenders of the traditional public pension arrangements. The review must examine the economic and social impacts of various pension approaches, assess how effective each is likely to be in ensuring adequate retirement incomes in an uncertain world, and identify the role that variations in social, cultural, and political traditions play in determining whether or not a particular kind of institution can prosper in a given environment. It should supply the foundation for an ongoing dialogue among the supporters of all approaches with the objective of developing a new consensus about the range of appropriate structures for national pension systems and the merits of following different approaches.

This volume is the initial step in the ISSA review process. It includes nine chapters that examine a variety of pension issues from an economic perspective. These chapters explore different aspects of the impact of pensions on the economy, the fiscal dynamics of different public pension approaches, and the challenges involved in ensuring that pensions provide adequate incomes. The review has begun with economic concerns because these are usually the basis for the strongest criticisms of existing pension systems and the major impetus for change in those systems.

The most common criticisms of pay-as-you-go pensions involve their economic impact, and that particular set of concerns is reviewed in the first five chapters of this volume. Pension systems, however, are not created because of the impact they might have on the macroeconomy. They are designed, first and foremost, to be mechanisms that provide retirement income to the aged population. This role is examined in detail in the issue briefs on the fiscal dynamics of public pension approaches and their adequacy as sources of retirement income.

For the most part, this volume leaves the social and cultural issues, which are also of great importance in the debate, for subsequent examination. These issues include the role of national pension programs as social institutions and the conditions under which different kinds of public and private institutions are likely to succeed or fail. These other topics are extremely important. The role that public pensions play in ensuring cohesion in a modern society is likely to be as important as any economic effect that they may have. In addition, history shows that serious problems with the operation of public pensions are frequently as much the result of institutional weaknesses as of design flaws. Designs that appear to work fairly effectively in one institutional setting can easily prove to be a disaster in another setting. These issues provide an agenda for future analyses as a part of this important ISSA initiative.

SUMMARY OF THE ISSUE BRIEFS

Chapter 2: Why Mandatory Retirement Programs Are Created

The logical starting point for this discussion is the question of why public pension programs exist at all. What purposes are they supposed to serve? What impact should we expect them to have? How should they be designed to achieve their purposes?

Both supporters and critics of the traditional pay-as-you-go pension systems agree that governments ought to require working-age people to make provisions for their retirement; they disagree about the most desirable mechanisms for achieving this. The agreement that some form of government intervention is necessary demonstrates a shared belief that free markets would not work properly to provide all citizens with adequate financial protection in retirement in the absence of government intervention.

One reason for government intervention is the desire to alleviate poverty, particularly among those no longer expected to work. As economies develop, extended family linkages weaken, and governments traditionally accept the responsibility of ensuring a minimum living standard for the aged. In many countries, public pension programs are the most important tool for discharging this responsibility, since they are effective in supplying at least a modest level of income to most aged and do so in a manner that preserves dignity and self-respect. Almost invariably, however, the scope and structure of the public pension program go far beyond the type of government effort that would be required just to provide a "safety net" to assure minimum living standards. It is this expanded scope that requires additional explanation.

The most common argument for this greater government role is that many working individuals who could adequately provide for their own retirement needs are myopic. In the absence of a government mandate, they would not have the foresight or discipline to save adequately for retirement. By the time they realized their mistake, it would be too late.

In effect, the government acts paternalistically to enforce a mandate that people may resent when they are young but will grow to appreciate as they get older.

A second argument is that the government mandate is required to protect the prudent members of society from free-riders. If, in the end, people believe that the government will ensure that all of the aged have access to a minimum living standard, some may make a conscious decision not to save on their own. To avoid having to pay both for themselves and for any imprudent neighbors, the prudent members of society force everyone to contribute.

A third argument focuses on the possibility of reducing the uncertainty involved when each individual is required to make his or her own retirement arrangements. Government interventions can reduce the difficulty of preparing for retirement in the face of uncertainty about the pace of future economic activity, the path of future investment returns and inflation rates, and the length of one's life.

Several observations about the structure of public pension plans flow from a review of these arguments. First, while the arguments suggest that some form of mandatory program is desirable, they do not suggest that the program must offer full earnings replacement for middle- and upper-income retirees.

Second, the arguments presume that many working-age people would not voluntarily make adequate provision for retirement. One key to successful implementation of a public pension program, therefore, is the willingness and ability of the government to enforce collections from reluctant individual and organizational contributors. One sometimes hears suggestions that compliance problems could be solved simply by linking benefits more closely to contributions. While such a change might have a beneficial impact, expecting it to produce a major increase in compliance would seem to ignore the basic assumptions about human behavior that motivated the creation of the pension program in the first place.

A third observation involves the likely impact of a public pension program on participant behavior. Public pension programs are designed to make it easier for people to retire at an "appropriate" age. The assumption is that, in their absence, people would have saved too little and thus been forced to work too long. It should be expected, then, that the implementation of a mandatory pension program will cause many participants to retire earlier than they otherwise would have, thereby reducing the labor force participation of the aged. To some degree, such an impact is the intended result.

Chapter 3: The Economic Cost of Pension Programs

The focus turns next to the fundamental economic issues underlying the public pension debate. Chapter 3 provides a careful examination of the factors that determine the actual economic cost of supporting the retired population. Chapters 4, 5, and 6 examine the likely impact of public pension systems on savings, labor force behavior, and international competitiveness.

One source of confusion about the economic impact of a public pension program can be traced to a failure to distinguish between the actual cost to the economy of the pension program and the social insurance contributions that are levied to finance those costs. Chapter 3 explores how changes in demography and public policies affect the economic cost of supporting the retired population. A later chapter explores how different economic and demographic environments cause the contribution rates required to finance pensions to rise or fall, even when the actual economic cost of supporting the retired has not changed.

The economic cost of supporting the retired population is best measured as the fraction of each year's total national economic activity that is devoted to supplying the goods and services the retired consume. This assumes that whatever part of the economy's capacity is used for this purpose cannot be used for some other purpose, such as producing consumer goods for the rest of the population or making new investments to increase future productivity.[1]

This economic cost is financed through some combination of transfers from the labor earnings of those who are not retired (usually in the form of pension contributions) and allocations of a portion of each year's returns to invested capital (usually in the form of earnings on assets owned by individual retirees or by pension funds). Different approaches to pension finance often involve different allocations of these costs between contributions and returns on assets. Confusion can occur when one approach appears to be cheaper than another because it involves lower pension contributions from earnings. If the lower charge to labor is offset by a higher charge to capital income, the total cost to the economy is the same even though it may be distributed differently.

The share of total economic activity devoted to the consumption of the retired—the actual economic cost of their support—is influenced by a variety of economic, demographic, and public policy developments. Perhaps the easiest way to understand how these various elements interact is to focus on the behavior of three key ratios: (1) *the aggregate consumption ratio*, which is the fraction of economic activity that is devoted to producing consumer goods and services for domestic use, (2) *the retiree dependency ratio*, which is the fraction of the population that is retired, and (3) *the living standards ratio*, which is the ratio of the average consumption of the retired population to the average consumption of all persons. When multiplied together, these three ratios will produce the ratio of retiree consumption to total economic activity, which is the economic cost of supporting the retired.

The relationship between changes in any of these three ratios and the corresponding change in the economic cost of the retired population is direct and proportional. Anything that causes one of these ratios to rise by a given percentage will increase the economic cost of supporting the retired by the same percentage. By the same token, *the cost of supporting the retired can only be reduced if changes that reduce at least one of these key ratios are introduced*.

As populations age, and if no other changes are made, the retiree dependency ratio will rise and the economic cost of supporting the retired will increase proportionately. The two most common adjustments that are discussed as ways of offsetting some of this cost increase are increasing the statutory retirement age, which would reduce the retiree dependency ratio, and reducing retirement benefits, which would lower the living standards ratio.

Shifting some or all of the responsibility for managing public pension plans from the public sector to the private sector has occasionally been advocated as a mechanism for reducing the cost of supporting the retired. Whether such a change has the desired effect depends entirely on whether it serves to decrease one of these key ratios. For example, if the shift is accompanied by changes that increase retirement ages or reduce the relative incomes of the retired population—or will be more effective at keeping retirement ages from drifting down or relative incomes from drifting up—it may well be an effective mechanism for reducing costs. If the shift is not accompanied by changes in dependency ratios or in the relative living standard of the retired, however, it will have no impact on the actual economic cost. Indeed, such a shift can actually increase the cost of supporting the retired if it produces higher retirement incomes. Higher incomes for the retired will most likely lead to an increase in their living standards relative to the rest of the population, causing the cost of supporting retired persons to rise.

Others advocate economic policies which they believe will accelerate economic growth as part of a strategy to deal with the rising cost of an aging population. While such policies may be desirable for other reasons, it is not at all clear that faster economic growth should be expected to reduce the economic cost of supporting the retired. If faster economic growth translates into more rapidly rising living standards of the working-age population *without having the same impact on the living standards of the retired population*, the *relative* cost of supporting the retired will drop. On the other hand, rising living standards among the working-age population may cause them to prefer earlier retirement and to offer less resistance to gradually rising pension contribution rates. Either reaction could mean that faster economic growth actually has the effect of increasing the cost of supporting the future retired population.

In summary, the economic cost of supporting the retired population is best measured by looking at the resources devoted to their consumption. Public pension benefit payments are a major source of support for the consumption of this population. For this reason, the best measure of the economic cost of a pension program is the benefits it provides. If it is important to prevent too great an increase in the costs of supporting the aged population, the evaluation of alternative policies to constrain these costs should focus on how effectively each will be in keeping pension benefit payments from rising.

PENSION IMPACTS ON THE ECONOMY

Even if the way that pension plans are financed is unlikely to have a significant impact on the share of national production devoted to supporting the retired, the financing approach may still have an important impact on everyone's living standards if it influences saving behavior, labor force behavior, or international competitiveness. Each of these three possible effects is discussed widely in the popular press, often as if the linkages were obvious and all of the impacts significant. Serious students of economics have been able to establish some, but not all, of the linkages. Where linkages have been found, many of the impacts appear to be relatively modest. These topics are explored in the next three issue briefs.

Chapter 4: Pensions and Savings

The relationship between pension finance and saving behavior has attracted the attention of economists for several decades and has produced a considerable volume of statistical studies. The primary issue has been whether pay-as-you-go pension systems reduce aggregate national savings and/or whether greater reliance on advance funded pension plans would increase national savings. If a consistent relationship can be found, pension policy changes could be used to increase aggregate national saving and produce a somewhat higher level of per capita economic activity.

Careful reviews that assess the whole body of recent analyses usually conclude that no consistent evidence exists which links the introduction of pay-as-you-go pension programs to declines in national saving rates. The linkage may well exist, but either it is too small to show up in the data or its impact is obscured by other factors.

In a similar vein, there is evidence (based largely on data from the United States) that the accumulation of assets in retirement accounts will cause total household saving to increase, though by less than the increase in the balances in the retirement accounts themselves. This positive effect from advance funded pensions appears to be either overshadowed or offset by the behavior of other components of national savings, however. Among these are the fiscal operations of government, business finance strategies, and customs and practices used to finance housing and other major consumer expenditures. At least among OECD countries, there is essentially no correlation between the rate at which pension assets have grown and the total savings rate in the economy.

All of this suggests that if higher saving is an important national goal, pension policy may have a role to play, but it is unlikely to have a discernable impact by itself. Pro-savings pension policies would have to be accompanied by other interventions such as a pro-saving tax code, government fiscal surpluses, and policies which discouraged consumer lending.

Several recent studies have found that the development of financial markets can provide an independent impetus to economic growth. Although the results are still controversial, they suggest that using advance funding for at least a portion of the pension system may have a beneficial economic impact independent of any impact on aggregate savings. The growing pension plans could provide a market for new financial instruments and help financial markets to develop.

Chapter 5: Pensions and Labor Supply

Public pension plans may also cause a reduction in productive economic activity through their impact on labor supply, the topic explored in this issue brief. One possibility is that mandatory pension plans may unduly discourage individual work effort both by lowering net pay during people's prime working years and by encouraging retirement when people reach the age at which benefits become available. Another is that they may encourage an artificial movement of people into less easily taxed, and often less productive, sectors of the economy if they force younger workers to set aside more for their retirement than these workers would prefer to do.

Studies of worker behavior offer some confirmation of the first concern. Pension contributions (and other earnings taxes) seem to have little effect on the work effort of those who are the primary source of support for themselves or their family. For those who have alternative sources of support, however, these studies find that social insurance contributions and other taxes on earnings do tend to reduce work effort at least somewhat.

The availability of pensions for older workers also seems to reduce work effort, especially among those whose health has deteriorated. Not surprisingly, there is a tendency for more generous pensions to have a more dramatic effect on work effort, although a change in the age at which pensions first become available would probably have a more powerful impact on retirement behavior than would a modest change in the amount paid at a given age. This means that if population aging forces pension retrenchments, a reduction in the monthly benefit payable beginning at a given age is as likely simply to produce lower retirement incomes as it is to lead to an increase in the average retirement age.

Since mandatory pension programs are established to require people to make more adequate provision for retirement, it must be assumed that their successful implementation will allow people to retire earlier than they would have without access to pension income. Current studies of labor supply impacts tell us that people do retire earlier than they would have without access to pension income. Since most societies have never articulated the social, political, or economic criteria for judging the impact of their policies, however, these studies are unable to tell us whether the actual impact is more or less than is desirable or if the benefits paid are too generous or not generous enough. We are also unable to say whether some discouragement of work effort among secondary earners is a reasonable price to pay for the gains that are secured when a pension plan is established.

Levying pension contributions creates an incentive for people either to hide from the tax collector in informal labor markets or to classify themselves as self-employed, since ensuring compliance among the self-employed has always been a challenge. By itself, reclassifying oneself as self-employed may have little impact on aggregate economic activity, although by reducing tax compliance it can create fiscal problems for the government and, depending on how closely benefits and contributions are linked, for the pension plan as well. Aggregate economic activity will suffer, however, if people seek out fringe employers in the informal labor market who operate in somewhat less productive sectors of the economy but who can offer a higher net wage by not paying pension contributions.

The situation can be particularly troublesome if the link between pension benefits and contributions is weak. In these cases, workers may be able to spend much of their careers in informal employment (or self-employment), escape the full payment of contributions, and still draw full pensions. In addition to any economic losses, such situations will cause major financial problems for the pension plan.

Pension systems in which the link between contribution payments and benefit receipt is as direct and clear as possible introduce fewer compliance disincentives and are better insulated from the financial problems associated with any remaining compliance problems. A close linkage should also help reduce any other labor market distortions. Some compliance problems should still be expected no matter how clear and close the linkage, however. If a clear and close linkage between contributions and benefits were sufficient by itself to produce near perfect compliance, there would be no need to have mandated the program in the first place.

Chapter 6: International Competitiveness

The recent slowing of economic growth in the industrialized world—and particularly in Western Europe—has caused concern that overly generous social security systems may be undermining international competitiveness.

It is generally acknowledged that well-designed social security programs can enhance international competitiveness by, for example, helping to smooth transitions from one industrial structure to another or facilitating worker movement to new employment opportunities. Poorly designed programs can discourage work effort, however, and even the best-designed programs can also be expensive. The question is whether the positive impact of these programs is being offset by the impact that financing them has on the cost of doing business in a particular country.

Economic theory suggests that the costs of running social security programs should not cause any particular international competitiveness problems where product markets, labor markets, and foreign exchange markets are allowed to operate fairly freely. In such an environment, any increase in pension contributions (or other social security charges) will translate into reductions in worker take-home pay rather than increases in the cost that businesses incur to hire labor, regardless of whether the contributions are collected initially from the employer or the employee.

Both labor market and international competitiveness problems can arise for an extended period of time, however, if some combination of government policies and labor market rigidities prevent the normal market adjustments to increases in social security contributions. When either government policies or private labor agreements prevent real wages from falling, an increase in employer contributions can cause business costs to rise and lead to increased unemployment. This situation can also cause international competitiveness problems if, in addition, either government policies or private capital movements prevent exchange rates from adjusting to trade imbalances, at least for a while.

Analysis of the relative competitiveness of different countries supports the view that social security programs can be beneficial to a country's competitiveness, but that high employer charges to finance them can be a problem. When OECD countries are ranked by their relative competitiveness, the more highly ranked tend to be those that spend a higher fraction of their GDP on social security. At the same time, higher employer contribution rates tend to be associated with somewhat lower competitiveness scores.

Choosing Among the Pension Approaches

The balance of the analysis undertaken in this volume focuses on some of the implications of choosing among the various approaches to providing mandatory public pensions. Chapters 7 and 8 examine aspects of aggregate pension financing: the relationship between pension approaches and contribution rates, and the challenges involved in changing from one approach to organizing public pensions to another. Chapters 9 and 10 focus on the adequacy of different public pension approaches for ensuring a predictable source of retirement income for individual participants.

Chapter 7: Setting Pension Contribution Rates

The economic cost of a pension program is best measured by looking at the relationship between aggregate benefit payments and total economic activity. However, the contribution rates needed to finance a given level of benefits may be higher under one approach to providing pensions than under another. The seventh chapter looks at the mathematics of pension contribution rates. It analyzes how economic, demographic, and institutional variables interact to cause differences in pension contribution rates, even when the actual economic costs of the pension program are the same.

Contribution rates under pay-as-you-go, defined benefit pension plans are set so that the aggregate receipts from all workers are sufficient to finance the aggregate benefit payments to all retirees. In these plans, contribution rates are sensitive to demographic changes but fairly insensitive to economic developments. A decrease in the number of contributors relative to the number of pensioners will force rates to rise, since the cost of financing a given quantity of pensions is spread among a smaller number of contributors. On the other hand, a change in prevailing earnings levels often has relatively little impact on the contribution rates needed to finance these plans, since any change is likely to cause more or less equal percentage changes in receipts and expenditures.[2]

Under the individual savings approach that is characteristic of most defined contribution plans, contribution rates need to be set so that each individual can accumulate financial assets of an amount sufficient to finance their desired level of retirement income. Since the financing plan focuses on the balance in each individual's account, declining birth rates (and the changes in the contributor/pensioner ratio that they induce) have no direct effect on the contribution rate calculation.[3] Contribution rates needed to obtain a specified level of retirement assets are determined instead by the interaction of interest rates (or, more generally, capital returns) and the rate of wage growth. An increase in the interest rate makes it easier to accumulate the necessary balance in retirement accounts and allows the system to operate with lower contribution rates. In contrast, an increase in the rate of earnings growth raises the amount of retirement assets that the pensioner must accumulate in order to finance a pension that will preserve the relationship between retirement income and pre-retirement earnings. This forces contribution rates to rise.

The relationship between contribution rates under funded, defined benefit pension plans and these particular economic and demographic variables is very similar to the response under individual savings approaches. In funded, defined benefit plans, contribution rates must be set so that sufficient assets are accumulated over the working life of each entering cohort to finance their retirement pensions. A major difference between these two approaches involves the ability of a group plan to smooth the impact that temporary changes in economics or demographics might otherwise have on each individual's pension. (This topic is explored more fully in the ninth chapter.)

Contribution rates under pay-as-you-go and funded plans are equally sensitive to changes in life expectancy at retirement. An increase in retiree life expectancy increases the amount that each worker must accumulate under an individual accounts approach, since the accumulation must last longer. It has the same impact on the amount that must be accumulated for an entire cohort of retiring workers under a funded, defined benefit plan. It also causes the ratio of contributors to pensioners to fall, thereby forcing contribution rates up in the pay-as-you-go approach. In all cases, the desirable impact on individual life prospects is accompanied by an undesirable impact on pension contribution rates.

The relationship between the pension contribution rates required under pay-as-you-go and funded approaches is fairly straightforward and predictable as long as one is operating in a simple world in which nobody dies before reaching retirement age and pension plans have no administrative costs. In such a world, relative contribution rates depend on only two numbers: the rate of population growth and the gap between the interest rate and the rate at which wages are growing. If the amount by which the interest rate exceeds the wage growth rate is larger than the population growth rate, the funded approaches will have lower contribution rates. If the gap is smaller than the population growth rate, the pay-as-you-go approach will have lower contribution rates.

One reason why the funded approaches have attracted more attention in recent years is that population growth rates have been falling and, at least in OECD countries, interest rates have been rising relative to wage growth rates for the last couple of decades. Assuming that both trends will continue into the future, the funded approaches will produce a given average pension with a lower contribution rate.

The relative attractiveness of the three basic approaches—pay-as-you-go defined benefit, funded defined benefit, and defined contribution—may change, however, when more realistic assumptions about mortality structure and administrative costs are introduced into the comparison. Defined benefit pension plans incorporate certain insurance features not found in defined contribution plans. When a worker dies in the years just prior to retirement, the pension obligations under a defined benefit plan are reduced, allowing the plan to be financed with a somewhat lower contribution rate. In contrast, preretirement mortality has no impact on the contribution rates required under the individual savings, defined contribution approach, since each account is financed on the assumption that its owner will survive.

Managing the accumulated financial assets causes administrative costs under advance funded plans to exceed those under comparable pay-as-you-go plans. Moreover, among advance funded plans, administrative costs are consistently higher under a system of individual accounts than under a group defined benefit plan, due to the loss of some economies of scale and to differences in marketing expenses. Finally, defined benefit plans automatically pay benefits in the form of life annuities, whereas holders of individual accounts must purchase annuities in order to achieve the same degree of assurance that their income will last for as long as they live. When purchased separately, annuities introduce another set of marketing and administrative costs.

These effects can cause the costs of running a defined benefit plan, particularly a pay-as-you-go plan, to be substantially lower than the costs of operating a defined contribution plan producing a similar retirement income. Depending on the particular demographic and economic conditions prevailing in a given society, the effects of early mortality and increased operating costs can amount to the equivalent of a 1.5 to 2.5 percentage point reduction in the annual rate of return earned on individual accounts.

Chapter 8: Changing from One Approach to Another

This chapter explores two important kinds of transitions that societies make in pension policies. First is the transition from having no public pension plan at all to creating a public pension plan. Second is the transition from one pension approach to another after a number of years.

The single most important reason for creating a pension program is to help ensure adequate incomes in retirement. This objective will be achieved much more rapidly under some approaches than under others, however, because the different approaches phase in at different speeds. Noncontributory programs phase in the most rapidly. Whether the program is income tested or universal, its adoption can quickly improve the income of all of the aged, including those retired at the time the program is initiated. Contributory, defined benefit approaches will be of no benefit to those already retired at the time they are instituted, but can be used to ensure adequate retirement incomes to those who are close to the retirement age as well as all who will follow. Defined contribution plans are the slowest to mature. They require over half a century to approach their full potential as a source of retirement income and are of limited benefit to anyone beyond the midpoint of their work career at the time they are instituted.

Because of the differences in the speed of maturation, the defined contribution approach is frequently not the option selected when a country is setting up its first public pension arrangements.[4] Over time, however, preferences about national pension policy are likely to evolve as systems mature and the pressure to assure adequate retirement incomes eases, and as economic, demographic, and social conditions change. For example, many countries which began by following one approach have subsequently broadened their strategy by combining several different approaches to form a mixed, or "multi-pillar," system. Contributory approaches are added to older, noncontributory approaches, and privately managed approaches are added where older systems were largely run by government. The new approaches frequently supplement and occasionally partially replace the earlier programs.

Many of these transitions occur gradually and relatively painlessly. Often, as income levels rise, the newer approaches are simply added in lieu of an expansion of the older ones. The added programs may be voluntary or they may be mandated.

The one transition that cannot be achieved gradually and painlessly is the transition in which a publicly managed, pay-as-you-go, defined benefit plan is replaced by a system of privately managed, advance funded, defined contribution accounts. The challenge is that the transition requires paying off the express and implied liabilities for future benefits under the pay-as-you-go system, while at the same time financing the new, defined contribution program. This involves duplicate payments which can easily be as much as 5 or 6 percent of a country's gross domestic product every year for several decades.

This kind of transition is difficult to justify on the basis of narrow cost calculations. Even if the transition payments are financed entirely through more government borrowing, under current economic conditions the additional cost just to service the new government debt is likely to be more than the cost of keeping the pay-as-you-go pension system in financial balance. For this reason, phasing out a social security system is usually not a very effective way of dealing with government fiscal problems, since it will likely make them worse for quite a few years into the future. Moreover, at least in principle, any positive economic impact that might be associated with such a change could have been achieved much more easily and with equal effectiveness by changing the benefit structure in the public system or by introducing a degree of advance funding to a system that had previously operated on a pay-as-you-go basis.

This type of transition may be justified, however, if it is the only effective way to solve certain political or institutional issues. It may provide the only politically acceptable way to reduce future benefit commitments, making it the most practical strategy for reducing the cost of supporting an aging population. It may also provide the most effective way for assuring that future benefit commitments don't grow beyond levels that the society can afford, or that assets accumulated to help pay retirement benefits are actually used for that purpose. In some societies, such a transition may be deemed the only practical way of assuring a reasonable quality of service to pensioners, or may be favored on general ideological grounds.

Chapter 9: Mid-Career Economic and Demographic Risks

Chapter 2 notes that one rationale for setting up a mandatory pension program is to give individuals a more predictable source of retirement income than they could obtain on their own. As has already been discussed, the amount that needs to be set aside each month (the contribution rate required) in order to accumulate a given volume of assets grows larger or smaller as investment returns fall or rise, but people in the earlier stages of their careers cannot predict future investment returns accurately. Moreover, the amount of assets that must be accumulated in order to assure a regular retirement income at a particular percentage of preretirement earnings depends on how fast earnings levels grow during the person's career and how long the person can expect to live once they have retired, which also are difficult to predict at the beginning of a career.

When a public pension program has been instituted, it promises (either explicitly or implicitly) that pensions will be available to those who make the required contribution payments. People measure the reliability of these promises in large measure by the degree to which a pension in the amount promised at the beginning of an employment career is actually available at the end of the career.

Pension promises are rarely realized precisely. Invariably, adjustments to earlier promises are required to reflect developments occurring during an individual's employment career. Chapter 9 explores how unexpected economic and demographic changes are likely to affect pension promises under each of the various type of public pension systems.

Pay-as-you-go, defined benefit plans generally have less risk of substantial benefit change than advance funded, defined contribution plans for two reasons, one related to the financing principle they employ and the other to the way benefits are set. Because of the way they are financed, the benefits provided under a pay-as-you-go plan are not nearly as sensitive to unforeseen economic developments, particularly changes in the rate of wage or price growth or changes in the rate of return on investments. This advantage is partially offset by the fact that pay-as-you-go approaches are more sensitive to changes in the rate of growth of the working-age population than are funded approaches. Historical evidence suggests, however, that sensitivity to economic changes is likely to be a more serious source of unpredictability than is a sensitivity to changes in the growth rate of the working-age population. The two financing approaches are equally vulnerable to changes in mortality experience among those who are retired.

When unforeseen problems do arise, prospective retirees under defined benefit plans are usually not required to absorb the entire impact of any necessary adjustment. Under defined benefit plans, unforeseen changes in economic and demographic conditions lead initially to an imbalance between receipts and expenditures rather than to a change in the promised benefits. Sooner or later, the imbalance is eliminated through some combination of benefit and contribution rate adjustments. Typically, the impact of correcting the imbalance is spread among current retirees, future retirees, and other contributors, with each absorbing a fraction of the total impact. In contrast, under the funded, defined contribution approach, all unanticipated economic changes are reflected fully in changes in the retirement assets and future retirement income of each participant.

Chapter 10: Post-Retirement Risk

Once individuals are retired they face two more kinds of uncertainty: unanticipated inflation and uncertainty about their own lifespans. These are the subject of the last chapter.

Traditional pay-as-you-go public pension programs all but eliminate both of these risks by paying benefits in the form of life annuities and adjusting the benefit amounts periodically to reflect changes in price or wage levels. The major risk that retirees bear is that benefit adjustments will be delayed or altered in the face of adverse economic conditions or unanticipated financial problems in the pension plan.

Dealing with these two sources of uncertainty is a somewhat bigger challenge under traditional defined contribution approaches, where retirees must support themselves for the rest of their lives by drawing down the stock of financial assets accumulated during their working lives. Where financial markets are reasonably well developed, both kinds of uncertainty can be reduced through the purchase of variable annuities. Absent some form of government intervention, however, the private market for variable annuities is likely to have two shortcomings: costs will be higher than under collective insurance schemes due to adverse selection problems, and the annuities will probably be indexed to financial market returns rather than to inflation or wage growth.

Governments can effectively remove these two problems by mandating that all retirees purchase annuities, thereby all but eliminating the risk of adverse selection, and by selling bonds whose principal and interest are indexed to prices, allowing the sale of private annuities whose benefits are indexed to inflation. However, both of these actions have drawbacks. In addition to possible philosophical objections, the disadvantage to mandating the purchase of annuities is that it may permanently harm cohorts who happen to reach retirement age at a time when the value of investment portfolios is temporarily depressed. The disadvantage of issuing indexed bonds is that they create for the government a pay-as-you-go liability which, though smaller than that associated with a pay-as-you-go public pension system, will be less amenable to modification in times of economic distress. Governments find it much easier to postpone or alter pension benefit adjustments than to postpone payments on bonds that they have issued.

GENERAL OBSERVATIONS

A number of concerns have been raised recently about the economic impact of pay-as-you-go, public pension programs. As one part of the

ISSA initiative, this both reviews these criticisms and also looks at several other important issues involving financial aspects of public pensions. This review supports several important observations.

First, certain elements of the economic critique that has been directed at traditional defined benefit, pay-as-you-go social security programs deserve to be taken seriously, but much of the criticism is either not supported by a careful review of current economic knowledge or seems overstated. Advance funding of public pension programs may yield economic benefits if pursued as one part of a plan for developing efficient financial markets. At the same time, there appears to be far less justification for assuming that advance funding will increase a nation's saving rate, and there is no reason to believe that it will reduce the economic cost of dealing with an aging society by itself.

If an increase in national savings is desired, advance funding of pensions might form one part of a much larger strategy, but the strategy needs to focus on the uses to which any additional funds supplied to capital markets are put as much as it does on using pension reform as a way to supply more funds. Moreover, taken by itself, even a large increase in national savings is likely to produce only very modest increases in real earnings levels.

One danger in focusing too much attention on how pensions are financed is that too little attention will be focused on a set of issues that is much more central to the challenge of dealing with the costs of an aging society. The economic cost of a retirement program is best measured by the benefit payments it makes; these benefit payments are also the major route by which the program affects the economy. If an aging society is causing these costs to rise to undesirable levels, adjustments will most likely require raising retirement ages and reducing retirement benefits. Changing the way pensions are financed changes the distribution of the costs, but doesn't necessarily change their magnitude.

The debate over social security and international competitiveness should be viewed as a debate about the balance between the gains from enhanced worker security and the losses from higher employer costs. It is a debate that deserves more careful analysis and less rhetoric than it has received thus far. In theory, free markets will ensure that the burden of social security contributions is borne by workers, regardless of whether contributions are initially levied against the employer or the employee. If this theory were always correct, the cost of social security programs would never affect international competitiveness. Scattered evidence suggests, however, that this theory does not necessarily describe what happens in the real world. Well-designed social security programs may actually work to increase international competitiveness, but part of the gain may be lost if they involve higher-than-average charges levied against employers' payrolls.

It is difficult to know what to make of the debate over the impact of social security on labor supply, largely because nations fail to address, either analytically or politically, the question of what the desired impact is supposed to be, and there is little if any evidence to suggest that different approaches to mandatory pension programs would have different impacts. Perhaps the best that can be said presently is that the picture is mixed. All public pension programs probably cause people to retire earlier than they otherwise would have, but that is why the programs were created in the first place. Unfortunately, no one seems to know how to address the issue of what the actual impact of pension programs on the work behavior of the aged ought to be.

Social insurance contributions, along with all other forms of taxes on labor income, probably cause some reduction in the work effort of members of the family other than the primary earner, and may encourage tax cheating in situations where the line between employment and self-employment is blurred or where enterprises are operating at the margin of the economy. A loose link between contributions and benefits can also cause financing problems for the pension plan. There is no evidence to suggest, however, that how a plan is financed (whether funded or pay-as-you-go) will alter the degree to which labor supply is reduced or tax cheating is encouraged. Each seems to be one of the costs that must be accepted as part of the price to be paid for the benefits secured through a public pension program.

Second, the economic critique has focused on the perceived shortcomings of the macroeconomic effects of the defined benefit model without paying sufficient attention to the relative merits of each pension model as an efficient device to supply retirement income. As a mechanism for supplying retirement income, the defined contribution model suffers from several marked shortcomings. The size of the retirement income stream produced is less predictable, while ensuring that retirement incomes last an entire lifetime and keeping benefits up to date with prevailing wage or price trends is more difficult. Individual defined contribution accounts have also proven expensive to administer, artificially increasing the economic cost of the retirement income system.

In a political system capable of exercising sufficient self-discipline, the defined benefit model also provides a more predictable source of retirement income and can be administered at a substantially lower cost. Neither of these advantages should be sacrificed unless there is good reason to believe that they will be more than offset by other kinds of gains.

A final observation goes beyond the material covered in the first phase of this review, but is necessary in order to complete the picture. As noted above, pay-as-you-go, defined benefit pension programs have many advantages when operated in the context of a political system capable of exercising sufficient self-control. History shows, however, that some political systems have not been able to operating such plans responsibly. They have allowed benefit promises to rise to levels that exceeded their society's willingness and ability to pay, creating serious fiscal problems for governments. Eventually these promises must be retracted, upsetting the retirement income expectations of people caught in the transition.

For reasons that go beyond the current review, this sort of political problem appears more common in some parts of the world and in some cultures than in others. Where it is a serious problem, the defined contribution approach is an attractive alternative because its benefits are more effectively insulated from political interference. Whether there are other institutional arrangements that would more effectively protect defined benefit plans from excessive political promises is currently unknown.

It is also too early to know how effectively the new systems based on the defined contribution model will be insulated from irresponsible behavior. Politicians are not the only people who are prone to promise more than they can deliver. The defined contribution model requires sophisticated oversight and regulation to ensure that one set of problems resulting from public sector political dynamics is not simply traded for a different set of problems derived from the dynamics of private sector operations.

The Future

This first phase of the ISSA initiative has been designed to foster a more careful review of the many complex economic and financial issues involved in constructing and reforming public pension programs. Subsequent phases will enrich the debate by expanding the focus to include additional social, political, and institutional dimensions. All are vital elements to be considered when constructing or reforming public pension programs.

Public pensions are critical institutions for a substantial portion of the population of many countries, and are destined to become even more important as population aging continues throughout the world. If conducted with care for the important viewpoints and dimensions, the debate over how these institutions should be structured will lead to a new and broader consensus about the role and shape of public pension programs. In turn, the emergence of a new consensus will ensure that changes introduced in the name of reform will strengthen these programs and make them better able to serve the millions who rely upon them.

Notes

1. Two other elements of cost could also be added: any reductions in GDP associated with the operations of pension programs and resulting from unintended changes in labor or capital markets, and costs associated with administering these programs. Each is discussed in later chapters.

2. The situation is slightly more complicated where, after retirement, benefits are adjusted for price increases rather than earnings increases. In that case, revenues grow in line with earnings whereas benefits grow in line with prices, and contribution rates can rise or fall if the two grow at different rates. Although this can be a serious issue for a few years during a severe recession, the effects tend to be far less dramatic over the longer run than are those of changes in birth rates.

3. Changes in population growth rates may have an indirect effect through their impact on prevailing real wage and interest rates. Such indirect effects are not considered in this analysis.

4. The most notable exception is the provident fund model of a group, defined contribution plan, which has been popular in many current and former members of the British Commonwealth.

Chapter Two

Reasons for Creating Mandatory Retirement Programs

Most countries adopt explicit policies to encourage the provision of retirement income as their economies develop. Mandatory, publicly managed retirement programs tend to emerge as wage-based employment becomes a more important source of economic support. At the beginning, they may cover primarily wage and salary workers in the public sector and in major transportation and export industries. Over time, however, they are usually extended to cover wage and salary workers throughout the formal sectors of the economy, and in some cases to virtually all of the economically active population. They are commonly financed, at least in part, through earnings-related contributions from covered employees and employers, and are often accompanied by public subsidies designed to encourage voluntary supplementation through private retirement programs.

These retirement programs are expensive undertakings. As economies mature, public pension programs grow to be among the largest fiscal institutions in their societies. Their financing typically requires worker (and/or employer) contributions in excess of 10 percent of gross earnings. Their financial flows can easily grow to represent some 5 to 10 percent of a country's gross domestic product, dwarfing virtually every other government activity.

Why do these programs exist? How can one explain such a widespread practice of imposing a substantial financial burden on a large fraction of the economically active population? Why do governments subsidize private sector retirement programs? Why were these programs created and what problems were they intended to address?

THE ROLE OF COLLECTIVE INTERVENTION IN A MARKET ECONOMY

Governments have long assumed some responsibility for ensuring a minimal living standard for the aged and infirm. In many countries, public pension programs have become an important mechanism for discharging that responsibility. These pension programs have grown well beyond the level needed to ensure a socially acceptable minimum, however, suggesting that the reasons for creating them go beyond the minimum income motivation.

A part of the explanation for this massive collective intervention must be found in the limitations of markets. Societies use markets to organize economic activity because markets generally assign economic resources to their most effective use. Markets have limits, though. Left to operate totally by themselves, they can fail to achieve important social objectives. For example, they offer no guarantee that a nation's borders will be secure or that its streets will be safe, they do a poor job of producing clean air and water, and they do not ensure the maintenance of minimal living and working conditions. Apparently, also, they can not be counted on to provide adequate retirement incomes. Thus, mandatory retirement programs are created and retirement program subsidies are provided on the assumption that they will improve social welfare.

Well-designed interventions can improve market outcomes if they effectively address instances where the market otherwise would fail. Such interventions can include regulations to control market actions and prevent certain market outcomes, subsidies or mandates to promote desired behaviors, and actual provision of goods and services. Each of these approaches can be found in the area of retirement income programs. Subsidies are used to encourage supplemental retirement programs, and regulations are used to limit the uses of funds placed in retirement accounts. Moreover, governments all over the world mandate participation in contributory retirement programs, which may be managed by the government itself, by the social partners, or by private profitmaking concerns.

Unfortunately, however, government interventions are not always well-designed and do not always improve the situation. Government's power can easily be used to produce outcomes that, though favorable to some, on balance are inferior to the market result. Programs favoring particular economic sectors or subsets of the population, including the aged, are particularly susceptible to being captured by the people who benefit from them, tailored to reflect the interests of the beneficiaries disproportionately, and expanded unduly. Moreover, even the best-designed and most desirable intervention is likely to introduce some undesirable side effects. These might involve extra costs associated with ensuring compliance with laws and regulations or artificial changes in the behavior of workers and investors induced by the existence of the taxes required to finance government activities.

Since collective interventions have the potential to either improve or worsen market outcomes, their structure and scope need to be considered carefully. Interventions should occur only when the specific reasons why the market is failing to function properly are clear, the consequences of not intervening are serious, the probability of successfully implementing corrective action is high, and any undesirable distortions created as part of the intervention are acceptable. Even when interventions are justified, their structure and scope should be appropriate to the problem they are to address, avoiding the natural tendency to grow too large or be used to unduly favor one or another segment of the population.

This chapter focuses on some of the reasons for and consequences of market failure and the implications of these for designing a retirement system. Other briefs in this series focus on the potential additional distortions introduced by retirement income systems, including possible impacts on the level of national savings, labor force behavior, and international competitiveness.

THE CAUSES OF MARKET FAILURE

People pass through several stages over the course of their lives. Years of economic activity are followed by retirement years, during which advancing age and deteriorating health make work more difficult, or at least less attractive. In principle, each individual can decide for himself how to divide consumption among these stages, saving in the earlier years in order to be able to continue consuming once earnings cease.

The near-universality of government action to change the outcome produced by such individual decisions suggests a general consensus that individual decisions and totally free markets cannot be counted on to produce a desirable level or pattern of saving for retirement. Analysts have suggested several reasons for such market failures. Four of the most common are: (1) individual myopia, (2) protection of the prudent, (3) income redistribution, and (4) insurance market failures.

(1) Individual Myopia

Myopia arises because some individuals give too little weight to the utility of future consumption when making economic decisions. For the purposes of this discussion, the concern is that the young would give inadequate consideration to their retirement consumption needs and save too little. As they grew older, they would realize the consequences of these earlier actions and conclude that they had made a mistake. They would find, however, that by the time they realized the mistake, it would be too late to rectify it.

Systematic errors of judgment such as this are not an important problem in many aspects of economic life. Most economic decisions occur in an environment in which consequences become apparent fairly quickly. If people do not like the consequences of past decisions, they make different decisions when the opportunity to decide presents itself again. In that way, any undesirable consequences of systematic errors of judgment are limited.

Retirement income decisions are unique. They are made early in life, but the consequences are not apparent until late in life. By the time people discover they made an error by not saving enough while working, they are no longer in a position to escape the consequences.[1]

An effective collective intervention to offset the effects of myopia will cause people to set aside more of their earnings during their working years so that they can afford a higher living standard during their retirement years. The intervention improves on the free market outcome to the extent that those approaching retirement age come to appreciate that the earlier intervention forced them to behave in a way that they now believe to have been appropriate.

(2) Protection of the Prudent

Governments have long assumed some responsibility for ensuring a minimum living standard for the aged and infirm. The existence of such a minimum, however, creates a moral hazard in that some members of society will decide to rely on the minimum benefit instead of making their own provision for retirement. The more generous this minimum level, the greater the risk. The prudent members of society are being taken advantage of because they must pay for both their own retirement and that of the imprudent. They can protect themselves by forcing all of those who might otherwise become eligible for the social minimum to make some contribution toward their own support in retirement.[2]

This particular market failure flows from the decision to provide a social minimum. It is not necessarily related to the presence or absence of myopia. Where a social minimum exists, being imprudent might be a perfectly rational response, especially for those whose resources in retirement are not likely to be significantly above the social minimum anyway.

In contrast to those who are myopic, the imprudent who are forced to make a larger contribution to their own retirements may never come to appreciate the wisdom of the government intervention. They would have preferred to remain imprudent. Since the intervention is designed to protect the prudent, it would be judged to be a success to the extent that few people who had adequate incomes during their working years ended up relying on the social minimum in their retirement years.

(3) Income Redistribution

Although markets generally do a good job in ensuring that economic resources are put to uses that have high social value, there is nothing particularly advantageous about the distribution of income that they produce in the process. Most societies make a collective judgment to alter the market-produced income distribution in order to promote greater social solidarity and produce a more just society. Common interventions include subsidizing education, supplementing the incomes of families with children, levying progressive taxes, imposing minimum wages, and offering social assistance to the low-income aged and infirm.

Pension programs (whether contributory or not) that are designed to favor those with lower lifetime earnings are one of the mechanisms a society can use to alter the market-generated income distribution. Compared to an assistance program, a pension program has the advantage of supplying income in a manner that preserves the dignity of the elderly because, in many societies, it is considered more socially acceptable. If the pension amount is kept relatively modest, it may also generate fewer savings disincentives among the working-age population than an assistance program would.

(4) Retirement Insurance

The young who prudently seek to provide for themselves in retirement must decide early in their careers how much to set aside in each work year in order to have sufficient resources for retirement. The challenge is that such decisions involve making projections about several developments that are unknowable. These include:

(a) The rate at which the economy will grow in the future and the future level and pattern of investment returns. Faster growth is likely to accelerate the rate of increase in earnings prior to retirement and increase the desired level of annual retirement income. In contrast, higher investment returns reduce the amount that must be set aside each working year in order to generate a given annual retirement income.

(b) Future trends in average mortality. An increase in the number of years that a particular birth cohort can expect to live after retiring increases the amount that all members of that cohort must set aside each working year in order to maintain a particular target living standard during retirement.

(c) Changes in price (or wage) levels after retirement. Unless provision has been made to offset their impact, such increases will erode the purchasing power of retirement income.

(d) Each person's lifespan, relative to that of the cohort as a whole. Absent offsetting arrangements, those who end up living longer than average will need to set aside more during each work year than those who end up with shorter-than-average lifespans.

Uncertainty about the impact of future events on an individual's economic status frequently can be addressed through the purchase of private insurance. Uncertainties of the type facing the individual retirement saver are not so easily handled by the private market, however.

The first two of these contingencies (economic growth and cohort mortality) can be addressed through the creation of "defined benefit" pension plans. These plans typically promise to provide a periodic benefit defined in relationship to earnings levels just prior to retirement. The risk of unanticipated changes in prevailing earnings levels, uncertain rates of return in the capital markets, and changes in cohort mortality are assumed, at least in theory, by the sponsor of the pension plan. In practice, where the plan is sponsored by a private employer, these risks are shared among future employees, customers, stockholders, and the government's revenue authority. The alternative pension model is the "defined contribution" plan, under which the pension is determined entirely by previous contributions and investment earnings. Under defined contribution retirement programs, these two risks are borne primarily by the individual, although governments may establish minimum guarantees that limit the individual's exposure.

Defined benefit arrangements may be provided voluntarily by private employers. However, absent a mandate either from the government or through collective bargaining, it is unlikely that all employers in a society would volunteer to sponsor such plans. Defined contribution plans can be sponsored by employers, but can as easily be established by each individual.

The third contingency (unanticipated inflation) can be insured against only by an institution whose resources adjust automatically when prices change. As a practical matter, in most countries this means that the government must supply the insurance, either by adjusting pensions directly or by issuing price-indexed government securities. When private insurers pledge to adjust payments for inflation, they usually back their promises with such government securities.

The fourth of these contingencies (individual mortality) can be addressed on an individual basis through the purchase of annuities. Where annuity purchase is entirely voluntary, the market for privately supplied annuities can experience serious adverse selection problems, which can limit its effectiveness. Such adverse selection problems are essentially eliminated (or reduced substantially), however, if all members of a retiring cohort are required to purchase annuities.

The implications of having individuals assume each of these risks are discussed elsewhere.[3] For the present, it is sufficient to note the following kinds of government interventions represent possible responses to limitations in private insurance markets: (1) mandates that ensure universal access to some form of defined benefit arrangement, which addresses the first two risks, (2) issuance of indexed government bonds, which ensure access to insurance against unanticipated inflation after retirement, and (3) mandates requiring universal purchase of annuities, which eliminates most of the adverse selection problem that otherwise limits the efficiency of insurance markets.[4] These government interventions are frequently accomplished by the creation of a publicly managed, defined benefit pension program that pays benefits as indexed annuities, but they can also be addressed through other strategies.

IMPLICATIONS FOR INTERVENTIONS

From this discussion of the reasons for collective intervention in retirement programs come several insights about how such involvement might be structured.

Scope of coverage. In principle, retirement programs ought to cover all forms of employment. Contributory pensions evolve in response to the perception that private markets would otherwise fail to provide an adequate income to those no longer able to work for pay. They are a practical option only where preretirement earnings levels are sufficiently high that some degree of self-financing of retirement is feasible. If intervention is desirable, it is likely to be just as desirable for private wage and salary workers as it is for government employees. It would also be desirable for those employed in the informal sectors of market economies, assuming that effective institutional arrangements can be developed for extending coverage to the informal sector and that those employed in that sector have sufficient earnings to make a formal retirement system possible.

Degree of compulsion. Addressing these market failures requires some combination of compulsion and subsidy. Myopia can be reduced through education, and myopic behavior can be reduced if retirement savings subsidies are offered. But, in the end, some degree of compulsion is probably unavoidable. The imprudent will not save even if subsidized, and the size of the subsidy needed to overcome the more severe cases of myopia may be unacceptably large. The market failures also imply the need for limitations on the rate at which benefit rights can be drawn down either prior to retirement or once retirement commences. The same forces that cause some individuals to behave myopically and encourage others to rely unnecessarily on minimum guarantees can easily cause each group to dissipate its retirement assets more rapidly than is socially desirable, if they are allowed to do so. Depending on the architecture of the retirement income system, some degree of compulsory participation may also be desirable in order to reduce adverse selection problems in private annuity markets.

Relative size of the mandatory element. None of the market failures discussed here implies that a government-imposed solution needs to attempt to deal with all of the retirement income needs of the aged. In each case, society might decide to require participation in programs that ensured everyone a reasonable retirement income base, but to leave to individuals a significant portion of the responsibility for ensuring the continuation of previous living standards, especially for higher earners. Governments often establish tax subsidies that encourage, but do not require, such voluntary supplementation. The case is clearest with respect to the need to protect the prudent. Dealing with that problem requires only a mandate sufficiently large to guarantee a retirement benefit equal to or greater than the minimum income guarantee provided to the aged.

The proper scope of the collective intervention to deal with the other three kinds of market failure will vary from one society to another depending on such factors as social and political traditions, relative strength of private and public sector institutions, and heterogeneity of the population. Mandatory programs necessarily apply to those who are prudent and far-sighted as well as to those who are imprudent or myopic. A program that effectively addresses problems of imprudence or myopia will very likely involve unwanted restrictions on the ability of the prudent and nonmyopic to provide for their retirement as they see fit.

As long as the mandatory programs are relatively modest, the undesirable consequences are unlikely to be serious. Retirement programs are quite popular among those receiving or about to receive benefits, however, presenting a constant threat of growth beyond the levels that can be justified by market failures. As mandatory programs become larger, they run a greater risk of introducing undesirable consequences, both for the economy and for individual choice.

Impacts on retirement behavior. One of the basic assumptions underlying mandatory pension policies is that, absent some form of intervention, myopic people will fail to make adequate provision for retirement. Consequently, they would reach retirement age with inadequate resources, requiring them to continue working longer (or seeking work) and eventually retire at a lower standard of living than would be the case in the absence of the market failure. Thus, successful intervention directed at offsetting myopia should produce both higher incomes for the aged and lower retirement ages. Interventions to improve the operations of insurance markets are likely to have similar effects, if only by making it cheaper and easier for people to finance their retirement.[5]

Impacts on personal saving. One purpose of intervention is to ensure that people enter retirement with adequate resources. Another is to ensure that they continue to have adequate resources even if they live well beyond the average life expectancy, have to deal with sharp and unexpected increases in prices, or face large expenses, such as nursing care. If the aged are left to deal with these risks on an individual basis, the prudent among them will have to accumulate additional savings (and spend these down more slowly in retirement) as a precaution. Programs that reduce these risks for the aged are likely to lead to some reduction in saving, at least among the prudent.

Implications for program structure. Much of the current debate about the size and structure of public pension systems focuses on whether they should be managed by the private sector or the public sector, and whether they should be based on the defined benefit model or the defined contribution model. In principle, market failures associated with myopia and the protection of the prudent can be addressed equally well through either defined contribution or defined benefit arrangements and can be managed by either the public or the private sector. Two of the four parts of the insurance motivation for intervention would be handled more easily through defined benefit arrangements than defined contribution arrangements. Only the government can ensure the socially desired level of income redistribution and effectively insure against unanticipated inflation.

SUMMARY

Totally free markets can fail to produce a socially desirable pattern of provision for retirement for at least four reasons. Two of the reasons, correcting for myopia and protecting the prudent, require some form of collective mandate or regulation but do not necessarily imply that retirement incomes must be supplied directly through government-operated programs. Also, neither of these two rationales necessarily implies that a mandated program must be sufficiently large to supply the majority of retirement incomes to the majority of the population, although the myopia rationale does not preclude that possibility.

The third reason, achieving redistribution through socially acceptable methods, requires either direct government operation or a program whose parameters are dictated by government mandate. But it does not imply a mandated program large enough to supply the majority of the retirement income to a majority of the population.

The fourth reason involves the desire to reduce some of the risks individuals would face in trying to make provision for retirement on their own. As a practical matter, the need for insurance against unanticipated inflation can be addressed only through government provision of indexed financial instruments, and private annuity markets are likely to operate much more efficiently if all retirees are required to participate, at least for a portion of their incomes. Reducing investment risks and the risk of changes in a cohort's life expectancy probably also require some intervention to ensure universal access to defined benefit pension arrangements.

The rationales for intervention apply to both the working years and the retirement years. The logic that suggests that the working-age population should be forced to set aside part of their incomes for retirement also suggests that retirees should be prevented from drawing down their accumulated benefit rights too rapidly. Moreover, a mandate that successfully causes people to consume less during their working years should be expected to have other effects on work behavior. In particular, higher retirement incomes and somewhat lower retirement ages may be taken as a sign that such a policy has succeeded. And some reduction in the amount of savings accumulated as a precaution against unforeseen events is the logical result of a program that reduces the risk or likely cost of such events.

NOTES

1. These ideas are not new. Pigou cites worker myopia as the justification for government intervention either to mandate or to subsidize provisions for old age. See A.C. Pigou, *The Economics of Welfare* (London: MacMillan, 1920). Feldstein bases many of his various analyses of the impact of social security on the assumption that a portion of the work force suffers from myopia. See, for example, Martin Feldstein, "Social Insurance," ed. Colin D. Campbell, *Income Redistribution* (Washington, D.C.: American Enterprise Institute, 1977), or Feldstein, "Social Security, Induced Retirement and Aggregate Capital Formation," *Journal of Political Economy* 82:5 (September/October 1974), 756–66. Diamond finds statistical evidence of systemic undersaving by a reasonable percentage of those approaching retirement age in the United States. See Peter A. Diamond, "A Framework for Social Security Analysis," *Journal of Public Economics* 8:3 (December 1977), 275–98.

2. This argument summarized here is developed in Feldstein, "Social Insurance," op. cit., in Richard Musgrave, "The Role of Social Insurance in an Overall Program for Social Welfare," ed. William G. Bowen et al., *The American System of Social Insurance* (New York: McGraw-Hill, 1968), 23–40, and in C. Eugene Steuerle and John M. Bakija, *Retooling Social Security for the 21st Century* (Washington, D.C.: The Urban Institute Press, 1994).

3. These implications are discussed in two other briefs in this series. One focuses on differences between defined contribution and defined benefit arrangements when earnings levels, investment returns, population growth rates, and mortality rates change during a work career. The other focuses on the implications for retirement income of both inflation and uncertain life spans.

4. Barr rests the case for government intervention in retirement provision largely on the inability of private markets to provide indexed annuities [see Nicholas Barr, "Economic Theory and the Welfare State," *Journal of Economic Literature* 30 (June 1992), 741–803]; Eckstein et al. focus on the imperfections in private annuity markets [see Zvi Eckstein, Martin Eichenbaum, and Dan Peled, "Uncertain Lifetimes and the Welfare Enhancing Properties of Annuity Markets and Social Security," *Journal of Public Economics* 26 (1985), 303–26]; and Diamond, op. cit., touches on all of the sources of insurance failure.

5. Note that in this case discouraging work (that is, encouraging retirement) is a sign that the program has succeeded in improving economic well-being.

Chapter Three

The Economic Cost of Supporting the Retired

The cost of retirement may be viewed alternatively from the perspective of the individual, the institution that manages a retirement benefit program, or the economy as a whole.[1] This chapter focuses on the cost as viewed from the third perspective, that of the economy. It begins with a discussion of the mechanisms used to ensure an adequate standard of living for the retired population. Next, it examines the factors that determine the aggregate amount of resources that will be used in any given year to support the retired, and how that aggregate can be changed. It concludes by looking at the potential impacts of shifting from public sector, pay-as-you-go approaches to private sector, advance funded approaches.

MECHANISMS FOR SUPPORTING THE RETIRED POPULATION

The sum total of the different kinds of economic activities undertaken each year is a set of goods and services used to support the private consumption of the domestic population, private investment, exports, or the government in what amounts to collective consumption or investment. This economic production process generates a corresponding flow of income to participants in the process. The aggregate income generated is equal in size to the aggregate amount produced.

Incomes generated in the process flow—in the first instance—to workers in return for their labor and to owners of the capital that was supplied. In a market economy, each, in turn, is able to consume a portion of the goods and services produced by using some or all of their income to purchase consumer goods in the marketplace. The goods and services consumed by the retired population must be produced more or less at the time they are consumed. Since (by definition) the retired population does not work, their consumption must be supported by means other than through labor income. There are only two possibilities. To the extent that the retirees are also the owners of capital, some portion of their consumption can be supported from the returns they receive on the capital they own. Otherwise, their consumption must be supported through transfers of resources from those who continue to work.

Taking into account the fraction of total capital income that must be reinvested in order to maintain the capital stock for future generations, and practical aspects of the way capital ownership is distributed among members of society, the retired population as a group is unlikely to be able to support itself entirely on current capital income.[2] Transfers of purchasing power from those who are not currently retired will necessarily represent a significant portion of the total means of support for the retired.

Societies employ various combinations of three different mechanisms for achieving the necessary transfers of purchasing power from the working age population to the retired: (1) informal, largely intrafamily transfers; (2) mandatory contribution and benefit (or tax and transfer) programs; and (3) asset exchanges. Virtually every society employs all three, although the relative importance of each varies across cultures and stages of economic development.

The first category involves transfers made voluntarily from those who are working to those who are retired. Its most common manifestation is the multiple-generation household in which the working-age members of the family support both the aged and the young. In a strict sense, the transfers may be "voluntary," but in reality they are usually backed by cultural traditions and social conventions which impose obligations as effectively as formal legislation. As societies become more urban, however, the multiple-generation household begins to break down, and sooner or later the role of intrafamily transfers shrinks while the role of one or both of the other mechanisms grows.

In effect, mandatory contribution/benefit programs, the second category, represent government assumption of the kind of activity that occurred more or less naturally in the first category. The need for a more formal social organization increases as mobility and rising income levels cause the breakup of multiple-generation households and declining birth rates reduce the number of one's own children (or even nieces and nephews) available for old age support.[3]

Government-sponsored transfer programs take one of two common forms: contributory (often earnings-related) pensions, and noncontributory universal pensions (or old-age assistance programs). Both are most commonly operated on a pay-as-you-go basis under which money flowing to the retired population comes in the form of direct transfers from the rest of the population. With contributory pensions, the transfer typically comes mostly from the labor income of current workers. Universal pensions are typically financed by more broadly based taxes so that the transfer comes out of both labor and capital income.

The third category, asset exchanges, involves transfers made through a *quid pro quo* arrangement. People accumulate something of value—precious metals, jewelry, real estate, or financial assets—during their working years and support themselves in retirement, at least in part, through the sale of these items. In general, the sales by retirees are to the young, who are themselves acquiring assets in anticipation of retirement. This is the essence of an advance funded, "capitalization" retirement system. The working-age population think of themselves as saving for retirement, even though most of their retirement saving is nothing more than the purchase of existing assets from the retirees. In this system, it is the act of purchasing the asset that creates the necessary transfer of purchasing power to the retiree.

All three of these mechanisms share a common attribute. The working-age population must reduce its own consumption below the level allowed by the share of its income generated by the production process in order to allow the retirees to increase their consumption to a higher level than their income from the production process would allow. The mechanism may be mandatory or it may be voluntary, it may be operated on a pay-as-you-go or on an advance funded basis, the consumption given up by the working age population may have been associated exclusively with labor income or with both labor and capital income, and the mechanisms employed may have either positive or negative side effects or byproducts. But the essential process of transfer is the same in all cases. Moreover, none of the mechanisms in and of itself increases the amount of resources available to society as a whole. They are all mechanisms for transferring ownership of the resources already created.[4]

THE ECONOMIC COST OF SUPPORTING THE RETIRED POPULATION

The economic cost of supporting the retired population is measured in terms of the goods and services that they consume. Regardless of how the retired population financed its purchases, goods and services consumed by the retired are not available for other uses.

The most useful measure of this cost is consumption of the retired expressed as a fraction of the total amount of production available to the society.

$$\text{Cost of Supporting the Retired} = \frac{\text{Consumption of the Retired}}{\text{Total National Production}^5}$$

In turn, this fraction can itself be expressed as the product of three other ratios:[6]

$$\text{Cost of Supporting the Retired} = \frac{\text{Total Consumption}}{\text{Total National Production}}$$
$$\times \frac{\text{Number of Retirees}}{\text{Total Population}}$$
$$\times \frac{\text{Average Consumption of Retirees}}{\text{Average Consumption of Total Population}}.$$

To put it another way, the cost of supporting the retired is simply the product of three different economic and demographic ratios:

(1) the *aggregate consumption ratio*, which is the fraction of total economic activity devoted to producing consumer goods and services;

(2) the *retiree dependency ratio*, which is the fraction of the population that is retired (which is going to be very similar to the aged dependency ratio); and

(3) the *living standards ratio*, which is the ratio of the average consumption of a retired person to the average consumption of all persons.

The fundamental factors that determine the cost of supporting the retired in any society are found primarily in the second and third ratios. The second ratio reflects the combination of the underlying age structure of the population and the social policies and practices governing the age at which people retire. The third reflects the social and economic conventions that govern the relationship between the living standards of the retired population and those of the population as a whole.

The relationships are simple and direct. A 10 percent increase in the fraction of the population that is over the age of retirement will lead, other things equal, to a 10 percent increase in the cost of supporting the retired. Likewise, a 10 percent reduction in the standard of living of the retired relative to the standard of living of the total population will lead, other things equal, to a 10 percent reduction in the cost of supporting the retired.

The three ratios also incorporate, in one way or another, all of the possible adjustments in the cost of supporting the retired. No society can alter the cost of supporting its retired population without pursuing policies that change at least one of these three ratios.

POLICIES TO ALTER THE COST OF SUPPORTING THE RETIRED

Much of the current debate over retirement policy is concerned with the impact of increases being projected for the future cost of supporting the retired. These increases are primarily the result of a projected aging of the population due to declines in birth rates and increases in longevity. Each has the effect of increasing the fraction of the population that is over a given chronological age, causing, other things equal, an increase in the retiree dependency ratio. For example, the OECD recently projected that the fraction of the population over the age of 65 in all member countries would rise from an average of 12.3 percent in 1980 to 21.0 percent in 2030, a 70 percent increase.[7] Without a change in either the age at which people enter retirement or the relative living standards of the retired, these demographic projections imply an equal 70 percent increase in the cost of supporting the retired (i.e., the fraction of total output going for this purpose) between 1980 and 2030.[8]

Few countries have begun to address the implications of these projections outside of their consequences for the financing of their public, pay-as-you-go pension plans. Where adjustments have been discussed (or enacted), they typically have taken one of three forms: changes in the retirement age in these public programs, adjustments in public pension benefit levels, or cost shifts from the public sector to the private sector.

Retirement age increases. If an increase in the statutory retirement age causes people to delay their retirement, the effect is to decrease the retiree dependency ratio. Offsetting the cost implications of the projected demographic shift entirely through increases in the retirement age is not likely to prove practical, however. The OECD projection noted above suggested an increase from 12.3 percent to 21.0 percent in the fraction of the population over the age of 65. In a world in which the total population is not growing and 21 percent of the population is over 65, the age that only 12.3 percent of the population exceeds is likely to be something like 73 or 74.[9] Roughly speaking, completely offsetting the increase in the aged dependency ratio requires that the qualifying age for all age-dependent benefits be adjusted upward by nine years relative to their position in 1980.[10]

Benefit reductions. Reductions in net pension benefits can reduce the cost of supporting the retired if they reduce the ratio of retiree living standards to those of the population as a whole. Policies of this type that have been adopted in public programs in recent years include increasing the rate of taxation on pension income, postponing scheduled increases in current benefits, changing the index used for adjusting current benefits, reducing accrual rates for future benefits, and adjusting the age at which "normal" benefits are paid without adjusting the age at which reduced benefits are paid.[11]

When the retiree dependency ratio rises, some reduction in retirement benefits is necessary to avoid having retiree living standards rise relative to those of the rest of the population. With no change in retirement benefits, the rise in the dependency ratio will lead to an increase in the rate at which income is transferred from the working-age population to the retired population, reducing consumption levels among the nonretired population. A corresponding reduction in retiree consumption levels would be needed, therefore, to preserve the relationship between the living standards of the two groups.[12]

Shifting costs to the private sector. Shifting costs to the private sector can be an effective way of offsetting the impact of aging on the public sector budget. Whether it also reduces the social cost of supporting the retired population depends on the impact that it has on one of the three ratios noted previously. If the shift is accompanied by reductions in either the relative living standards of the retired population or that population's relative size, the shift will also reduce the share of the total production that goes to support the retired. On the other hand, if incomes of the retired are increased relative to those of the rest of the population, the switch could have the effect of reducing the cost to the public budget but increasing the total cost to society of supporting the retired.

The Impact of Moving From Pay-As-You-Go To Advance Funding

Projections of the impact that an aging population is likely to have on public, pay-as-you-go pension programs have prompted a great deal of interest in shifting some or all of the pension responsibilities of these plans to advance funded approaches, frequently managed by the private sector. As is discussed in chapter 4, such a shift may benefit the economy as a whole either through its impact on aggregate savings or through its encouragement of the development of efficient financial markets.[13] It is difficult to predict whether the shift would also reduce the economic cost of supporting the retired population.

The impact of a shift from pay-as-you-go to advance funding on the economic cost of supporting the retired will depend, in the end, on the effect it has on one of the three ratios outlined previously.

How costs might be reduced. Shifting costs to the private sector can help reduce the cost of supporting the retired if it facilitates retrenchments in either benefit levels or retirement ages. This could occur either because such retrenchments were an explicit part of the reform package or because reform created a set of institutional arrangements which were more effective in resisting pressures for benefit expansions.

Several of the Latin American countries that have recently shifted a significant amount of the responsibility to the private sector have been able to incorporate increases in retirement ages and reductions in the future value of past benefit accruals in their reform packages. Each of these changes will reduce the cost of supporting the future retired population. Sponsors of these reforms also believe that the new approaches create institutional arrangements which will prove substantially more effective in preventing unsustainable expansions in future benefits than the public sector arrangements they replaced.

How costs might be increased. The most important possible offsetting influence involves the risk that new arrangements might increase retirement incomes by more than they increase aggregate economic activity. Advocates of shifting from pay-as-you-go, public programs to a system of privately managed, individual accounts often argue that such a change will offer the working-age population a greater return on their pension contributions.[14] If this turns out to be true, future retirees are likely to have larger pensions than would have been the case without the reform. Unless these larger pensions are offset by proportionately higher incomes among the working-age population, however, the living standards ratio will rise, causing the economic cost of supporting the retired to rise also.

INCREASING THE RATE OF GROWTH OF THE ECONOMY

A common element in debates over pension policy is the interest in institutional changes that might increase the rate of growth of the total income available for supporting the retired. Among the possibilities often cited are increasing the rate of capital formation, encouraging the development of more efficient financial markets, and removing distortions in the labor market. If effective, reductions in labor distortions would cause a one-time increase in the total amount produced in the economy. Economists are not agreed about whether improvements in the capital markets would also produce only a one-time increase or could lead to a permanent increase in growth rates. Even if enhanced growth from such a change were not permanent, however, the change might increase the growth rate for several decades.

Many other economic reforms having nothing to do with pension institutions also have the potential to increase the rate of economic growth. Presumably, the impact of faster economic growth on the economic cost of supporting the retired would be the same, regardless of whether the accelerated growth can be traced to changes in pension institutions or to other economic changes.

An increase in the growth rate will increase the total amount of goods and services available for allocation among the various competing uses and consumers. The impact of an increase in the rate of economic growth on the share of total production going to support the retired population is less clear, however. A change in the rate of economic growth will change the allocation of total production only if one or more of the three ratios noted previously also changes. Several kinds of adjustments to one or more of the ratios are possible.

Depending on how the institutions that produce retirement incomes actually adjust, an increase in the growth rate might reduce the cost of the retired population through a reduction in the living standards ratio. For example, if retirement incomes are set with reference to living standards prevailing at the time of retirement (or earlier), an acceleration in the rate of growth of the economy would cause the living standards of the working-age population to rise by more than those of the retired population. The living standards of the retired population would fall relative to those of the working-age population, but would not decline in absolute level. In this way, the share of output going to the retired would also decline.

It is also possible, however, that faster economic growth would lead to an increase in the share of output going to support the retired. This could happen through the impact that higher real incomes might have on retirement preferences. A richer society might decide to use a part of its wealth to purchase earlier retirement for itself, causing an increase in the retiree dependency ratio. Faster growth is also likely to reduce the degree of resistance to increases in the taxes or contributions needed to finance higher retirement pensions. With faster growth, it is easier for the government to divert a slowly rising fraction of the gross income of the working-age population to other purposes without preventing them from continuing to experience rising living standards.

SUMMARY

Societies employ various combinations of three different approaches for transferring income from the working-age population to the retired population: voluntary, largely intrafamily arrangements, public programs collecting revenues through mandated contributions or general taxes to finance pension or other assistance payments, and individual-based exchanges of assets between retirees and workers (exemplified by arrangements under which retirees finance their consumption through the sale of financial assets to the working-age population). All three approaches require a reduction in the amount the working-age population could otherwise consume so that the retired can consume more than would be possible if they had to rely exclusively on their current earnings and investment returns.

The share of total production going to support the retired population can be expressed as the product of three ratios: the *aggregate consumption ratio*, the fraction of total economic activity devoted to the production of goods and services, the *retiree dependency ratio*, the fraction of the population that is retired, and the *living standards ratio*, the ratio of the average consumption of the retired to the average consumption of all persons. All changes in the share of output going to support the retired must be reflected in changes in one or more of these ratios.

Over the next several decades, most of the developed world (and many developing countries) will experience a significant aging in their populations due to lower birth rates and longer life expectancies. Without offsetting changes, this will lead to sharp increases in the relative cost of supporting the retired (the fraction of total economic activity devoted to the consumption of the retired population) through its impact on the retiree dependency ratio. One manifestation of the increase in this cost is the projected increase in the contribution rates required under virtually every public sector, pay-as-you-go pension plan.

Much of the current debate over pension policy revolves around the question of how to deal with the cost of the projected aging of the population. One set of policy prescriptions involves changes in public programs designed to lower the future ratio of the consumption of the retired to the consumption of the total population. These include increases in the retirement age (which reduce the retiree dependency ratio) and reductions in retirement benefits (which reduce the living standards ratio).

Shifting to greater reliance on private sector institutions to support the consumption of the retired can either increase or decrease the relative cost of supporting the retired. If the shift is accompanied by reforms that increase retirement ages or reduce relative living standards or if it is more effective than public approaches at keeping retirement ages from drifting down or the living standards ratio from drifting up, such a shift can be an effective mechanism for reducing costs. If the shift ends up producing higher retirement incomes, however, it will cause the cost of supporting the retired to rise even more.

The impact of faster economic growth is also ambiguous. If faster economic growth translates into more rapidly rising living standards of the working-age population without having the same impact on the retired population, the cost of supporting the retired will drop. On the other hand, rising living standards among the working-age population may cause them to prefer earlier retirement and to offer less resistance to the increasing of pension contribution rates. This would increase the cost of supporting the future retired population.

Notes

1. The first perspective involves examining what each individual must put away during working years to finance his or her own retirement. The second involves examining what each particular institution that has assumed part of the responsibility for providing support to the retired (such as employers or the government) must pay each year to finance the benefits they have promised. The third involves examining the fraction of total economic activity that will be devoted to supporting the consumption needs of the retired.

2. Even if the income flows were large enough, developing the institutional arrangements necessary to ensure that capital ownership (i.e., the right to the capital income) shifted smoothly among individuals strictly in accordance to whether or not they were retired is likely to prove an insurmountable challenge.

3. The same demographic trends which cause formal retirement systems to become more expensive also make them more necessary.

4. Note, also, that all mechanisms operate on the implicit assumption that another generation will come along to keep the chain going. Even a strategy that relies on asset exchanges must have successor generations in order to function, since the assets have value only if there is somebody else who will purchase them.

5. Technically, the consumption measure refers to consumption of domestically produced goods and services. In addition, the aggregate measure "gross national product" is more appropriate for this purpose than the more common "gross domestic product." The difference is that the former includes the returns on foreign assets owned by a country's nationals and excludes returns on domestic assets owned by foreigners. In cases where such flows are quantitatively important, the treatment in the gross national product formulation more nearly approximates the resources available to support the domestic retired population.

6. Those interested in the more formal derivation of these relationships are referred to Annex 1.

7. Organization for Economic Cooperation and Development, "Aging Populations, The Social Policy Implications" (Paris: OECD, 1988). The figure is an unweighted average.

8. Each nation will have to decide for itself how it wishes to adjust to this increase. The same projections suggest that the higher cost of supporting the retired will be offset partially by lower costs of supporting the young. They show the population under age 15 declining from 22.9 percent in 1980 to 17.2 percent in 2030. Numerically, the decline in youth dependency offsets roughly two-thirds of the increase in age dependency. The impact on economic costs is likely to be somewhat lower, however, since per capita consumption tends to be lower for children.

9. Calculated from the U.S. life table for women born in 1920, under which, assuming a constant population, roughly 21 percent would be over the age of 65 and 12 percent would be over the age of 74. This calculation is only illustrative. The age of equivalence will depend on the rate of growth of the population as well as the exact structure of age-specific mortality rates.

10. If rising age dependency ratios lead to labor shortages (a hypothesis which appears more credible at this time for Japan and North America than for Europe), countries may adapt by importing guest workers or liberalizing immigration policies. Each would effectively reduce the retiree dependency ratio. The longer-term impact of such policies depends on the obligations incurred to support the retirement of the immigrants or guest workers.

11. An increase in the "normal" retirement age, which leaves unchanged the age at which benefits can first be taken and which also reduces proportionately the amount that is received at the age of first eligibility, is probably more accurately characterized as a benefit reduction than as an increase in the retirement age.

12. As a simple example, consider a pay-as-you-go pension which produces a benefit equal to 50 percent of the average gross wage while working and requires a 10 percent contribution rate. This pension is actually replacing 55.5 percent of wages net of pension contributions (0.5 divided by 0.9, the ratio of net wage to gross wage). If adverse demographic developments cause the contribution rate to rise to 20 percent and no adjustment is made in the pension benefit, retirees would be advantaged relative to workers because their pension would now equal 62.5 percent of net wages (0.5 divided by 0.8). In this example, preserving the original relationship between the pension income of the retirees and the net wage of the workers requires that the pension be reduced to a little over 44 percent of gross wages (0.555 × 0.8).

13. This issue is explored more fully in the accompanying brief on the effect of pension plans on savings and investment.

14. This issue is explored in the accompanying brief on the mathematics of pension contribution rates.

APPENDIX I

Algebraic Derivation of the Relative Burden

Assume:

- C = aggregate consumption
- CR = aggregate consumption of retirees
- N = total population
- R = total number of retirees
- Y = total income

Then:

(1) aggregate consumption ratio = C/Y
(2) retiree dependency ratio = R/N
(3) average retiree consumption = CR/R
(4) average total consumption = C/N
(5) living standards ratio = average retiree consumption divided by average total consumption
  = $(CR/R)/(C/N)$
  = $(CR/R)(N/C)$

Since the relative burden is the product of the three ratios numbered previously as (1), (2), and (5):

relative burden = $(C/Y)(R/N)(CR/R)(N/C)$.

The following appear in both the numerator and the denominator, and therefore cancel out: C, N, and R.

This leaves the relative burden as CR/Y, the fraction of total income used to support the retired population.

Chapter Four

The Effect of Pensions on Saving and Investment

The impact of pension operations on national saving and investment is one of the most hotly debated topics in pension policy. An adequate level of effectively planned investment is a key ingredient in improving future living standards. Saving generates the resources that can finance that investment.

The relationship between pension policy and investment is of interest for two quite different reasons. One is a concern that while national pension programs may have succeeded in their goal of ensuring adequate retirement incomes, they have had the undesirable side effect of reducing national saving and investment. The fear is that the social gains from more adequate retirement income are being offset—at least partially—by the social losses associated with less investment and slower growth.

A second reason to focus on the relationship between pensions, saving, and investment is the desire to use changes in pension arrangements to generate additional saving or improve the efficiency of investment patterns, without regard to any impact that current pension arrangements may have had on saving. In this case, the goal may be to increase saving and investment *above the levels that would have prevailed in the absence of any government pension arrangements*. Presumably, those who advocate these kinds of policies need to explain why the level of saving produced by the operation of the free market is inadequate, demonstrate that changes in pension policies are likely to result in increased saving rates, and establish that such changes will not also reduce the effectiveness of the pension system as a mechanism for providing retirement income.

Opinions differ about the possibility of structuring pension policies to encourage productive investment without sacrificing other important social objectives. Part of the dispute involves questions about the strength of any connection between pension policy and investment. If the linkage is weak, pension policy may not be an effective way to encourage investment. Another part of the dispute involves the compatibility between pension structures that seem to encourage investment and those that help achieve the other important social objectives that pensions were established to achieve. Structures that might encourage investment are less attractive if they also require substantial sacrifice of other social objectives.

THE LINK BETWEEN SAVING AND GROWTH

Economies grow because of increases in the amount of labor and/or capital employed and through increases in the productivity of each. Investment is the process through which capital is accumulated. Investment increases the amount of capital available for each worker to use and facilitates the introduction of new, more efficient production techniques.

Investment is possible only if the amount of resources used for domestic consumption is reduced or capital can be imported from abroad.[1] Saving is the process through which domestic consumption is reduced and provides the chief engine for investment. But the link between the saving behavior of an individual and national investment flows is complex and not always clear.

First, national saving is the sum of the net saving of a country's households (usually called personal saving), its businesses, and its governmental units. An increase in saving among households will actually translate into higher national saving only if it is not accompanied by an offsetting reduction in either business or government saving. For example, a particular change in a country's tax laws might encourage individuals to save more, which would increase national saving in the absence of any other changes. But the tax change might also cause a deficit in the government's budget, which would mean that government was dissaving. Unless the increase in household saving was larger than the increase in the government deficit, the net effect of the change in the tax law would be to reduce national saving.

Second, saving occurs only when the net effect of a set of transactions is a reduction in total consumption. A particular household may save for retirement by reducing its consumption and making a deposit in a financial institution. One cannot know whether this transaction translates into higher national saving, however, without knowing what use was made of the funds deposited in the financial institution. If these funds are loaned to a business establishment to finance a new facility, they have added to national saving and helped finance new investment. On the other hand, the transaction will produce no increase in net saving or investment if the funds are loaned to another working-age household to finance the purchase of a new car or other consumer item, loaned to the government to finance a budget deficit, or paid out to a retiree who is supporting himself by drawing down the balance he had accumulated in the same financial institution.

Third, economic growth can be enhanced only if any increase in national saving gets translated into productive investment. In particular, macroeconomic conditions must encourage investment or else higher saving may cause a near-term economic contraction instead of the desired longer-term increase in economic capacity. In addition, available investment funds must be allocated to productive uses. Political interference in investment decisions, imperfections in domestic capital markets, or any number of internal structural barriers may cause investment funds to flow to less productive uses, limiting the impact of higher saving on future economic health.

This chapter focuses primarily on the relationship between pension structure and national saving. It will also note the current discussion of a possible linkage between economic growth, the structure of financial markets, and pension reform. It will not attempt to cover in any detail other issues related to the management of the macroeconomy or the efficient use of investment funds.

The major part of this chapter explores what is known about the relationship between pension institutions and household (or personal) saving. This is the particular topic that has traditionally received the most attention. The chapter then looks at the relationship between pension institutions, government saving rates, and a nation's total saving rate. Even though it is the linkage between pensions and national saving that is the key to understanding how pension policy affects investment, that particular link has not been explored as extensively. The chapter closes by looking at possible links between financial markets and economic growth.

How Pensions Affect Personal Saving: Predictions from Economic Theory

Unfortunately, it is not possible to predict the likely impact of pensions based solely on our understanding of the general operation of the economy. Economic reasoning reveals that several forces may be at work. These forces push in conflicting directions and their relative magnitude cannot be known in advance. Major elements of the economic logic are outlined in this section. The statistical evidence is explored in a subsequent chapter.

The lifecycle theory of consumption. Over the past four decades, the starting point for most analyses has been the lifecycle theory of consumption. According to this theory, individual saving behavior is geared to closing gaps between the timing of expected income receipts and the timing of desired consumption expenses over the course of the lifecycle. In particular, savings are accumulated during the working years and drawn down during retirement years.

The lifecycle theory predicts that, in the absence of government intervention, a nation's accumulated stock of savings (its aggregate wealth) at any given time will be determined largely by the age structure of its population and its retirement patterns. Wealth increases as people save for retirement and declines as they draw down their retirement savings. The size of the wealth stock at any time depends on the relative size of the two flows. It will tend to grow if the working-age population is large relative to the retiree population, but will decline if the retiree population rises without a corresponding increase in the working-age population.

Increases in the rate of growth of the economy will also lead to increased saving rates. When they expect higher future earnings levels, workers will increase the amount they set aside for retirement to assure a corresponding increase in their retirement income. Finally, if workers decide to increase the fraction of their lifetime spent in retirement, they will increase their saving rates; if they decide to work longer, saving rates will fall.[2]

Other theories of consumer saving. The implications of the lifecycle model are often adjusted to reflect the impact of several other theories. Two have particular importance for discussions of national pension policy. The first is that a measurable fraction of aggregate household saving may be motivated by the desire to bequeath wealth to one's heirs. A second is that an important motivation for saving is the uncertainty about consumption needs in the future, in particular about how long one will live and what extraordinary expenses (particularly medical and long-term care expenses) might arise near the end of one's life.[3]

The potential impact of introducing a national pension plan.[4] The impact of a national pension plan depends on how individuals change their saving behavior when the plan is introduced. As a starting point, economists assume that people will view the mandatory contributions to a national pension plan as a substitute for at least a part of their own personal saving and the future benefit they expect to receive as a substitute for some or all of the retirement dissaving that would otherwise occur.

If people actually behaved this way, logic would dictate that the introduction of the pension plan would have *no effect on aggregate saving so long as all of the following conditions held*:

(1) the mandatory contributions were less than or equal to the amount each person would have saved in the absence of the pension plan;

(2) the relationship between benefits paid under the plan to each individual and that individual's contributions (i.e., the rate of return that can be expected) mirror the relationship the individual would have experienced in the private marketplace;

(3) the pension plan accumulates and invests assets in the same way as the individual would have; and

(4) the creation of the plan has no effect on the desirability of saving to deal with future uncertainties.

Of course, no national pension plan meets all four of these conditions. Indeed, *no purpose would be served by creating a plan that met all four of these conditions*. Such a plan would produce a result that would have been achieved anyway by the private market. National pension plans are designed intentionally to depart from one or more of these conditions precisely because societies wish to alter the private market result. But what impact might these intentional departures have on national saving?

Effect of higher mandatory contributions. Presumably, a mandatory pension plan will require contributions in excess of the amounts that some in the working-age population would have set aside voluntarily. These higher contributions force the affected individuals to reduce current consumption, and, in the absence of an offsetting effect, their reduced consumption would increase national saving.

One possible offset to the higher saving involves the workers' ability to borrow. If credit markets allow them to go deeper into debt, they can offset the impact that the national pension plan would otherwise have on their consumption levels.

An additional possibility is that the forced participation in the national pension system encourages people to plan on retiring earlier and with a higher total retirement income than would otherwise have been the case. This encourages them to increase their private saving in order to supplement their national pension benefit, thereby increasing national saving.[5]

Effect of the relationship between benefits and contributions.[6] Most national pension systems offer some individuals benefits that are higher than they would have been able to obtain in the private market with the same contributions. These are typically lower earners and those already in the labor force at the time the plans were established. They may also be persons employed in particular occupations or industries that have been afforded special treatment.

Others can expect to receive less from the national pension system than had they made the same contributions to individual savings accounts. Typically, this would include higher earners who have spent most of their careers working under the pension plan. In many mature national pension plans, the majority of newly entrant workers can now expect to find themselves in this situation.[7]

Those who would otherwise allocate their lifetime earnings according to the pattern implied by the lifecycle theory will change that allocation if they find themselves in either of these two groups. The former group, those who foresee returns in excess of the private market rate, can be expected to increase their consumption during their working lives in recognition of the higher expected retirement benefit. Increased consumption implies reduced national saving. The latter group, those who foresee returns below the private market rate, can be expected to increase their saving during their working years in order to replace some portion of the retirement income they lost as a result of being forced to participate in the retirement income system.

The net effect of differences in the relationship between benefits and contributions will depend on the relative strength of the offsetting reactions of these two groups. In countries with mature national pension systems, the net effect ought to be an increase in national saving owing to the larger size and higher income of the latter group. The net effect is apt to be a net reduction in saving where national pension systems are relatively new and are structured so that most current participants can expect above-market returns.

Effect of differing asset accumulation patterns. One significant difference between most national pension programs and any private saving they have displaced is that the former tend to be operated more or less on a pay-as-you-go basis, whereas the latter are, by definition, advance funded.

During the start-up phase of an advance funded system, contributions are made but almost no benefits are paid. Instead, the contributions finance the accumulation of wealth. Only after the system matures are most of the retired population able to support themselves by drawing down their accumulated retirement assets. In contrast, under a classic pay-as-you-go system, early contributions are collected at a lower rate and are used to finance higher benefit payments to the initial retirees. As the system matures, the pay-as-you-go contribution rate rises to approximate—or even exceed—the contribution rate necessary under advance funding for the same level of pension.

In principle, the advance funded approach should generate additional national savings during the start-up phase through two mechanisms, the higher initial contribution rate required of the employed and the lower benefits paid to retirees. Each reduces aggregate consumption relative to the situation under the pay-as-you-go approach.

Several theories that might substantially narrow the differences between the pay-as-you-go approach and the funded approach have been advanced. One involves possible offsets operating through the pattern of bequests. If the working-age population reacts to the introduction of a pay-as-you-go system by increasing the volume of bequests, the greater savings needed to generate these bequests can offset partially the lower savings otherwise associated with starting a pay-as-you-go system.[8] A second complication can arise if, as a practical matter, the alternatives to a government-sponsored pay-as-you-go system are privately operated pay-as-you-go systems, such as those produced through informal intrafamily arrangements or more formal systems associated with fraternal or occupational organizations.[9]

Effect on incentive to save for uncertainties. National social welfare programs reduce many of the uncertainties that people face in planning for retirement. National pension plans normally pay benefits as life annuities, reducing the uncertainty associated with not knowing how long one's assets must last. In developed market economies, these benefits are often indexed to reduce uncertainties associated with future inflation. Most countries offer the aged, if not the entire population, comprehensive assurance that needed health care will be provided, further reducing retirement uncertainties. And some countries have formal systems for handling the long-term care needs of a frail population. All of these policies enhance social welfare by increasing the security of the retired population. They also reduce the incentive that people might otherwise have to save in advance to cover these contingencies.

Summary of possible effects. In summary, economic reasoning does not lead to a clear prediction about the impact of a national pension system on personal saving.

Introduction of a national pension plan is likely to *increase* national saving to the extent that it forces people to make higher contributions for their retirement programs than they would otherwise make, encourages people to retire earlier than they otherwise would, or offers people a lower return than they would receive on individual retirement savings.

Such an introduction is likely to *reduce* national saving to the extent that it offers people higher returns than they would receive on individual retirement savings, replaces advance funded retirement arrangements with pay-as-you-go arrangements, and effectively reduces the risks associated with not knowing how long one will live or what future inflation rates might be.

Finally, a national pension plan might *have little effect* on saving to the extent that it codifies the arrangements that would have existed in its absence (including private, pay-as-you-go arrangements), people are able to offset any forced saving that might otherwise occur by increasing their borrowing, or any change in the liabilities of future generations is offset by changes in the volume of bequests from current generations.

HOW PENSIONS AFFECT PERSONAL SAVING: STATISTICAL EVIDENCE

Attempts to measure the actual impact of pension plans on saving behavior face a number of challenges that analysts have so far not successfully overcome. Comparisons that focus on aggregate national saving either look at trends over time in one particular country or at differences at a point in time among different countries. In either case, the available data are imperfect and the ability to adjust for the influence of other factors is seriously limited. A frustrating consequence is that two researchers can each produce studies that convincingly convey contradictory findings. Slight variations in the particular way a statistical test is conducted, the particular way that other influences are accounted for, or the particular set of years or sample of countries studied can mean the difference between finding that social security programs increase saving, reduce saving, or have no effect at all.[10] Studies that look at variations in saving behavior among individuals in a particular country suffer from other statistical limitations and are unable to generalize from the possible effects on one part of the population to the impact on total national saving.

Studies of the impact of pay-as-you-go pension plans. In many countries, national pension plans now operate largely on a pay-as-you-go basis, regardless of whether they were originally designed with that approach in mind. By far the most common premise for statistical studies has been the examination of whether such approaches have had the unintended effect of reducing national saving.

Unfortunately, efforts to establish the relationship between pay-as-you-go pension plans and national saving rates have not been successful. After an exhaustive review of cross-country studies and studies of the potential impact of the system in the United States, one noted American economist concluded:

> For a variety of reasons, ranging from introspection and personal experience to the analysis of statistics on saving, people have developed hunches about how social security affects saving. Economists, who are no more immune to hunches than anyone else, have applied the tools of their discipline to try to determine which of these hunches is correct.
>
> The evidence is conclusive that so far they have failed. Using the best that economic theory and statistical techniques have to offer, they have produced a series of studies that can be selectively cited by the true believers of conflicting hunches or by people with political agendas that they seek to advance.[11]

Reviewing the evidence ten years later, the World Bank reached much the same conclusion:

> . . .numerous empirical investigations (most of them based on U.S. data) have been unable to prove conclusively that saving did, indeed, drop once pay-as-you-go programs were established. . . . Analysis of saving rates in other countries yield similar conflicting results. Studies of the saving impact of old age security programs in Canada, France, the Federal Republic of Germany, Japan, Sweden, and the United Kingdom found no significant impact, except for a slightly positive aggregate effect in Sweden, where the pension program is heavily funded.[12]

Studies of the impact of advance funded plans. Even if pay-as-you-go plans have not reduced saving, switching to advance funded plans could increase saving. As noted previously, such a policy might be pursued because of a concern that, without government intervention, the free market would generate inadequate saving. Mandatory, advance funded pensions are a form of government intervention that has the potential for altering this result.

Only a handful of studies have explored systematically the possible impact on national saving of advance funded pension or retirement arrangements. All of these studies focus on the experience in the United States and Canada.

One category of studies examines programs that offer tax subsidies to encourage individual retirement saving. They explore the extent to which such policies cause people to save more or simply cause people who had already saved to switch their assets into tax-favored accounts. No clear conclusion emerges from the studies.[13]

Other studies have focused on whether the asset holdings of individual households vary systematically with variations in their prospective pension entitlements. They also focus on the experience in the United States and Canada, where private pensions are often a part of the employment package but are not required by law. These may or may not be representative of the situation in other societies and under a universal mandatory scheme.

The question being researched in these studies is whether households scheduled to receive higher pensions appear, relative to their income levels and holding other things constant, to have smaller holdings of other financial assets. To the extent they do, the smaller holdings can be assumed to be offsetting some of the increased saving that would otherwise result from the asset accumulation occurring in pension funds. These studies tend to find evidence of partial offset. Perhaps 60 percent (results commonly range between 40 percent and 80 percent) of the assets accumulated in pension funds are not offset directly by reduced asset accumulation among recipient households.[14] Since pensions in the United States and Canada are more common among higher-wage firms, the degree of asset offset under a universal pension plan might be even lower. Lower earners have less ability to make offsetting reductions in personal asset holdings.

Summary of statistical evidence. Despite numerous attempts to measure the impact statistically, no consistent evidence has emerged linking the creation of pay-as-you-go social security systems with reductions in personal saving rates. This suggests that if these programs have had a negative impact on personal saving, it probably has been a fairly modest one. At the same time, studies also suggest that advance funded plans can lead to an increase in personal savings, though by less than the gross amount of the assets accumulated in these plans. Although pay-as-you-go pensions may not be responsible for depressing personal saving, relying instead on advance funded approaches may nevertheless cause personal saving to rise.

The Link Between Personal Saving and National Saving

Generalizations are even more difficult when the perspective is broadened to include potential links between pension policies and total national savings. The limited evidence available suggests that the positive relationship between advance funded pensions and personal saving rates may not carry over into a positive relationship between advance funding and the national saving rate. On the other hand, while pay-as-you-go pensions may themselves have had little impact on either personal or national saving, attempts to maintain the broader welfare state may have reduced national saving through its impact on government budgets.

As noted previously, the positive relationship between advance funded pensions and personal saving will translate into increased national saving only if the fact that funds are flowing into pension plans does not trigger offsetting changes in either the government budget or the economy's financial liabilities. Unfortunately, both kinds of offsetting changes are possible. In most countries, deferred pension income is taxed more lightly than is ordinary saving. Thus, any switch in the holding of assets away from individuals and toward pension plans will reduce the government's tax revenue and lead, other things equal, to an increase in government borrowing. Also, increases in financial assets held by private pension funds need not necessarily lead to higher saving in the economy if they are used to finance additional consumption rather than additional investment. National saving does not rise if pension managers use their funds to finance credit card debt.

Data describing recent experience in several OECD countries show no clear relationship between the accumulation of assets in private pension funds and national saving rates, suggesting that these kinds of offsets may have been occurring. OECD countries differ widely both in the prevalence of advance funded pensions and in levels of national saving, as can be seen in table 1. A comparison of saving rates over the decades of the 1970s and 1980s with the rates at which pension assets grew during each decade in each country (charts 1 and 2) suggest essentially no correlation between the two.[15]

In an extensive review of OECD saving patterns, Dean, Durand, Fallon, and Hoeller analyze a number of factors that appear to account for some of the differences among the countries and time periods.[16] They note the role that the growth of public pensions may play. But they also present evidence of the impact of a number of other factors, including variations in demographic patterns and trends, increases in consumer credit due to financial market liberalizations, unanticipated inflation, changes in housing and equity prices, tax policies, and real interest rates. Any differential impact from the growth of pension plan assets may simply be lost in the interaction of all of these influences.

Table 1: Growth in Private Pension Assets Relative to Gross National Savings, 1971–1991

Country	Gross Savings (% of GDP)		Pension Assets (% of GDP)			
	1971–80	1981–88	1970	1980	Change (1970–80)	1991	Change (1980–91)
Canada	23.1	20.3	14.2	18.7	4.5	35.0	16.3
Denmark	20.3	15.0	18.8	26.3	7.5	60.0	33.7
Germany	23.7	22.2	2.6	2.6	0.0	4.0	1.4
Japan	34.4	31.4	0.0	3.2	3.2	8.0	4.8
Netherlands	23.9	22.3	29.0	46.0	17.0	76.0	30.0
Switzerland	28.0	28.4	38.0	51.0	13.0	70.0	19.0
U.K.	17.1	16.8	20.7	28.1	7.4	73.0	44.9
U.S.	19.5	16.1	29.3	40.7	11.4	66.0	25.3
France	25.4	19.8	0.0	1.0	1.0	3.0	2.0

Sources: Dean, Durand, Fallon, and Hoeller, "Saving Trends and Behaviour in OECD Countries," OECD Economic Studies 14, (Spring 1990), table 1, 14; Averting the Old Age Crisis (World Bank, 1994), table 5.2, 174.

At the same time, recent OECD data also suggest that government fiscal policies may play a major role in national saving trends. Table 2 reproduces data from the same article by Dean, et al., showing changes between the 1960s and the 1980s in the national saving rates of a number of OECD countries and how those changes are divided between changes in government saving and changes in private sector saving. Although national saving rates declined substantially between the 1960s and the 1980s in almost all OECD countries, in most of these countries virtually all of the decline is associated with deterioration in the fiscal conditions of government.

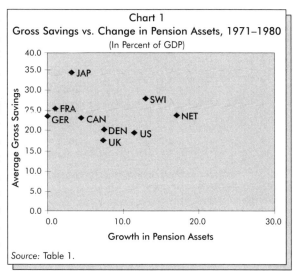

Chart 1
Gross Savings vs. Change in Pension Assets, 1971–1980
(In Percent of GDP)

Source: Table 1.

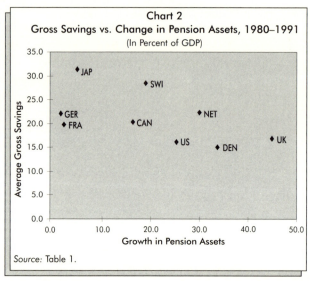

Chart 2
Gross Savings vs. Change in Pension Assets, 1980–1991
(In Percent of GDP)

Source: Table 1.

The fiscal problems experienced by most OECD governments since the mid-1970s arose, at least in part, from pressures to maintain social welfare spending in the face of deteriorating economic conditions. To the extent that those pressures can be traced either to challenges in meeting past pension promises or to the consequences of tax incentives to encourage retirement saving, part of the responsibility for the decline in government saving may appropriately be attributable to pension policies. Indeed, it may be that pension policies affect national saving as much through their impact on the government budget as through any direct adjustments they trigger in private saving rates.

Table 2: Change in Average Savings Ratios Between 1960–1970 and 1981–1987
(In Percent of GDP)

Country	National	Government	Private Sector
U.S.	-3.3	-4.2	1.0
Japan	-3.9	-2.0	-1.9
Germany	-5.5	-4.4	-1.1
Italy	-5.4	-7.3	2.0
U.K.	-1.7	-4.3	4.6
Canada	-1.5	-5.9	4.4
Austria	-4.2	-4.6	0.3
Belgium	-7.4	-7.9	0.6
Finland	-1.8	-3.6	1.8
Norway	0.8	1.0	-0.2

Source: Dean, Durand, Fallon, and Hoeller, "Saving Trends and Behaviour in OECD Countries," OECD Economic Studies 14, (Spring 1990), table 3, 19.

A similar story emerges in another study that focuses only on the experience in Sweden but carefully traces the interactions of personal, business, and government behavior after the introduction of a partially funded, earnings-related public pension in 1960. The evidence suggests some reduction in both personal and business savings that was offset, at least in the initial years, by the increase in government savings. Problems developed, however, when the public sector began to find itself overcommitted in the late 1970s.[17]

POTENTIAL GAINS FROM HIGHER SAVING

Several analysts have developed quantitative estimates of the potential economic gain from changing national pension programs in a way that they believe would lead to increased national saving and investment. These estimates assume that the kind of offsetting adjustments just discussed will not occur in the future. They suggest that under these circumstances major changes in pension policy might have measurable but rather modest impacts.

Martin Feldstein calculates that changing the current pay-as-you-go social security program in the United States into one based on funded, individual accounts would eventually increase the aggregate capital stock by about 25 percent. But he further calculates that an increase of this size in the capital stock would lead to only a 5.7 percent increase in GDP.[18] Since the changeover would occur over a period of 50 years or more, the calculation implies an acceleration of about 0.1 percent per year in the rate of growth of GDP.

Kotlikoff, Smetters, and Walliser assume that a similar change in the structure of the social security program of the United States would have an even larger impact. They find that after 70 years have elapsed, the change has produced a 37 percent increase in the capital stock which, they calculate, will generate an 11 percent increase in GDP. In their simulation, however, all of this translates into an increase of only 3.7 percent in real wage levels.[19] Cifuentes and Valdés-Prieto simulated the impact of two proposed Hungarian pension reforms and found that the proposal involving greater reliance on advance funding might increase future GDP by some 8 percent, whereas the proposal that relied on pay-as-you-go financing might produce an increase of only about 1.5 percent of GDP.[20]

EFFICIENCY OF FINANCIAL MARKETS

A related debate among financial economists involves whether altering pension institutions can have a positive impact on economic growth for reasons not directly related to their effect on national saving. The issue is the relative advantage of relying primarily on the banking sector as the source of outside capital for a nation's private business enterprises (the traditional practice in Japan and continental Europe) as opposed to relying on independent financial intermediaries and equity markets (the traditional practice in the United States and the United Kingdom). Independent financial intermediaries are said to be more receptive to financing new enterprises and imposing financial discipline on older, inefficient enterprises. On the other hand, they are also said to impart an undesirable short-term bias to financial decisionmaking.[21]

Those who believe that the use of independent intermediaries is more likely to foster economic growth may see in the creation of advance funded pension accounts a means to facilitate the emergence of financial markets, especially in transition economies that did not previously have such markets. The argument would be that the form of the pension institution may affect economic growth indirectly through its impact on financial markets even if it has no direct effect on saving rates.[22] Research on this issue is fairly recent. The experience of those countries implementing reforms needs to be monitored for evidence of the existence and magnitude of these possible positive effects.

Summary

Economic reasoning cannot be relied upon to conclude that a national pension system will have a particular impact on national saving. Systems that offer low implicit returns on contributions and systems that encourage people to retire earlier or to make higher contributions than they would otherwise prefer may well increase saving. Systems that give people higher returns on their contributions, encourage later retirement, reduce the risks associated with living in old age, or substitute pay-as-you-go arrangements for advance funded arrangements may well reduce saving.

Statistical studies have not been very helpful in resolving controversies about the relationship between saving rates and pension plan structure and finance. Those who have examined in detail the whole range of studies of the impact of pay-as-you-go systems on saving seem to agree that these studies do not support the conclusion that national saving rates have declined as a result of the introduction of pay-as-you-go pensions.

An advance funded pension system ought to have a more favorable impact on national saving rates than a pay-as-you-go system, at least during the start-up phase. Studies do suggest that the assets accumulated in such pension plans are not entirely offset by the action of participating households, but the statistical evidence does not afford a very clear picture of the net impact on the economy as a whole of advance funded pensions.

Studies suggest that pension policy is only one of many factors influencing national saving rates. Policy changes designed to increase saving probably need to deal comprehensively with a variety of factors, including tax policy, fiscal policies, and credit market policies. Such policies may also include changes in the way pensions are organized and financed, especially if pension policies can be adjusted to promote greater saving without unduly sacrificing other important retirement income objectives. The statistical evidence is not of sufficient quality, however, to justify adopting a particular pension approach deemed to be inferior on other grounds solely in the hope that it will increase national saving rates.

Notes

1. Foreign capital is imported whenever a country runs a deficit in its international trade accounts. In effect, foreigners have shipped more goods and services to the country than they have taken out of it, leaving the country able to utilize more goods and services that year than it produced domestically. Foreign capital flows will be ignored in the balance of this chapter, since it is concerned with the impact of pension policy on the ability of a country to finance its own investment.

2. See Franco Modigliani, "Life Cycle, Individual Thrift, and the Wealth of Nations," *American Economic Review* 76 (June 1986), 297–313; and "The Key to Saving Is Growth, Not Thrift," *Challenge* (May–June, 1987), 24–29. Note that the lifecycle theory implies that it is higher growth that produces higher saving whereas popular discussions seem always to assume the reverse, that the higher savings are causing the higher growth. Perhaps both are true.

3. For example, Laurence J. Kotlikoff, "Intergenerational Transfers and Savings," *Journal of Economic Perspectives* 2:2 (Spring 1988), 41–58. These two supplemental theories may help explain why the aged appear to dissave less and wealth appears to be distributed less equally among the population than the lifecycle theory would seem to imply.

4. National pension plans raise money to finance benefit payments through either taxes or mandatory contributions. For ease of exposition, the discussion here assumes a model of earnings-related benefits financed entirely by earmarked social insurance contributions, although the results also apply to other models.

5. The effect could only occur among those individuals (or in those countries) where the benefits under the national pension system are insufficient to fully support retirees so that they need to supplement the public pension benefit if previous living standards are to be maintained [for example, Martin Feldstein, "Social Security, Induced

Retirement and Aggregate Capital Accumulation," *Journal of Political Economy* 82:5 (September–October 1974), 756–66].

6. This topic is analyzed more completely in chapter 7.

7. See, for example, C. Eugene Steuerle and John M. Bakija, *Retooling Social Security for the 21st Century* (Washington, D.C.: The Urban Institute Press, 1994) or "Issue Brief 2: Pay-As-You-Go or Fully Funded: Which Costs Less?" The World Bank, *Averting the Old Age Crisis* (Oxford: Oxford University Press, 1994), 297–302.

8. For example, Robert J. Barro, "Are Government Bonds Net Worth?" *Journal of Political Economy* 82:6 (November-December 1974), 1095–117.

9. This point may have little relevance for today's developed economies but may still apply in parts of the developing world where family and informal arrangements remain important. After analyzing the finances of then-existing craft-based pension arrangements, Pigou concluded that introducing a national pension insurance scheme in the United Kingdom was likely to have only a modest effect on capital formation for this reason. See A.C. Pigou, *The Economics of Welfare* (London: MacMillian, 1920). See also the discussion of informal retirement income systems in The World Bank, op. cit., Chapter 2.

10. Leimer and Lesnoy demonstrate this point for time series studies in the United States. [See Dean R. Leimer and Selig D. Lesnoy, "Social Security and Private Saving: New Time Series Evidence," *Journal of Political Economy* 90 (June 1982), 606–42.] Barro and MacDonald look at cross-country comparisons and conclude, ". . .any desired sign for the social security variable in a cross-country. . .equation can be picked by judicious choice of specification. . ." [See Robert J. Barro and Glenn M. MacDonald, "Social Security and Consumer Spending in an International Cross Section," *Journal of Public Economics* 11 (June 1979), 287.]

11. Henry J. Aaron, *The Economic Effects of Social Security* (Washington, D.C.: The Brookings Institution, 1982), 51.

12. The World Bank, op. cit., 307. Knut Magnussen of Statistics Norway has compiled what is probably the most thorough and careful current review of studies of the impact of social security on saving. [See Knut Magnussen, "Old-Age Pensions, Retirement Behaviour and Personal Saving," Discussion Paper PI-9609 (London: The Pensions Institute, Birkbeck College, University of London, August 1996).]

13. These particular studies—along with others addressing more generally the relationship between social security and saving—are summarized in Gerard Hughes, "Pension Financing, the Substitution Effect and National Savings," paper for an international conference on "Pensions in the European Union: Adapting to Economic and Social Change," organized by the European Commission, DG V, and Gesellschaft für Versicherungswissenschaft und-gestaltung e.V., Münster, Germany, June 1996.

14. This literature is summarized in Alicia H. Munnell and Frederick O. Yohn, "What Is the Impact of Pensions On Savings?" ed. Zvi Bodie and Alicia Munnell, *Pensions and the Economy: Sources, Uses and Limitations of Data* (Philadelphia, Penn.: The University of Pennsylvania Press, 1992); in K.A., Magnussen, op. cit.; and in Gerard Hughes, op. cit.

15. This analysis follows the lead of Gerard Hughes, op. cit.

16. Andrew Dean, Martine Durand, John Fallon, and Peter Hoeller, "Saving Trends and Behaviour in OECD Countries," *OECD Economic Studies* 14 (Spring 1990), 7–59.

17. Edward Palmer, "Public and Private Pensions and Saving in Sweden," *Conjugating Public and Private: The Case of Pensions, Studies and Research* 24 (Geneva: International Social Security Association, 1987).

18. Martin Feldstein, "The Missing Piece in Policy Analysis: Social Security Reform," *American Economic Review* 86:2 (May 1996), 1–14.

19. Laurence J. Kotlikoff, Kent Smetters, and Jan Walliser, "Privatizing U.S. Social Security—A Simulation Study," paper presented at the World Bank Conference on "Pension Systems: From Crisis to Reform" (Washington, D.C.: November 1996). These results assume that the transition is financed through increases in consumption taxes. Other strategies for financing the transition produce somewhat less favorable results.

20. Rodrigo Cifuentes and Salvador Valdés-Prieto, "Fiscal Effects of Pension Reform, A Simple Simulation Model," paper presented at the World Bank Conference on "Pension Systems: From Crisis to Reform" (Washington, D.C.: November 1996).

21. See, for example, Ajit Singh, "Pension Reform, the Stock Market, Capital Formation and Economic Growth: A Critical Commentary on the World Bank's Proposals," *International Social Security Review* 49 (1996), 21–43.

22. For example, Holzmann finds that improvements in the financial markets in Chile added something over 1 percent per year to the growth rate. Some portion of these improvements is probably attributable to the pension reform there. See Robert Holzmann, "Pension Reform, Financial Market Development, and Economic Growth: Preliminary Evidence from Chile," IMF Working Paper 96-94, (August 1996.)

Chapter Five

The Effect of Pensions on Labor Supply

Pension programs can affect individual labor supply decisions through both the benefits they provide and the contributions levied to finance those benefits. Each has the potential for causing undesirable effects. A desire to evade pension contributions may encourage individuals to seek employment in sectors of the economy where enforcement is lax but labor productivity is lower. Both the benefit and the contribution requirements may produce an unintended reduction in people's general willingness to work. These kinds of economic distortions artificially increase the cost of supporting the retired population by reducing the productive capacity of the economy.

Assessing the labor supply impact of public pension programs involves two kinds of challenges. One is the limitations in data, statistical techniques, and behavioral theories that complicate the task of understanding the actual link between pension plan provisions and worker behavior. The other is the need to differentiate between the impacts that are intentional and desirable and those that are not.

Mandatory pension programs are established for the express purpose of changing how labor markets operate. In particular, the objective of a mandatory pension program is to allow people to retire earlier and/or with higher retirement incomes than would otherwise be the case. If a pension program achieves this result and has no other impact on labor markets, then any reduction in labor supply that it causes must be viewed as producing an increase in social welfare.[1] Economic costs arise only when the levying of contributions creates distortions or the benefit provisions inadvertently produce an unintended change in individual behavior.

This chapter reviews the current understanding of the link between pension provisions and labor supply. It begins with a discussion of the insights from economic theory about the possible relationships. It then reviews the statistical evidence that has been developed in recent years and discusses some of the policy implications of this evidence.

How Pensions Affect Labor Supply: Predictions from Economic Theory

As with saving behavior, it is not possible to predict in advance how the creation of a mandatory pension system will affect labor supply. The impact will depend, among other things, on the time horizon over which people make decisions, the structure of the pension plan, popular perceptions about how the pension plan is managed and financed, social norms, and which of two potentially offsetting economic forces influencing worker behavior is the stronger.

A good starting point in sifting through these various influences is with the question of whether the pension plan is viewed primarily as a system of forced savings or simply as an unrelated set of government taxes and benefit payments.

Unrelated taxes and payments. If people view a public pension program as simply an unrelated set of government-imposed taxes and government-provided benefit payments, its impact on labor supply will come from the independent influence that the payment of contributions has on the behavior of the working-age population and that the receipt of benefit payments has on the older population.

In this situation, the deduction of social insurance contributions from a worker's gross earnings reduces the net remuneration from working each hour. How this affects work effort depends on which of two conflicting influences is the stronger, as well as on the effectiveness of enforcement. In one way, these deductions provide an incentive to work. Since net earnings from each hour of work are reduced, more hours of work are needed to produce the same take-home pay. In another way, however, the deductions constitute a work disincentive. Since the net gain from working an additional hour is smaller, there is less incentive to find a job or work a little longer on the one currently held.[2] The presence of these deductions also creates an incentive to seek employment in parts of the economy either where their imposition is not required under the law or where the law is poorly enforced.

Under most situations, the impact of the payment of benefits is less ambiguous. They increase the income of the recipients, allowing recipients to reduce their work (that is to say, to retire) without suffering as great a reduction in take-home pay. Additionally, when the payment of benefits is conditioned on a specific kind of behavior, they will also encourage that behavior. In particular, if benefits are not paid to those who continue to have earnings above a certain level, people will be encouraged not to have earnings above the specified level. In both cases, work effort is discouraged.

Benefits and contributions linked. Where people view a pension program as more closely resembling a program of forced savings, any labor supply impacts among the working-age population should be substantially reduced. In fact, the pension system should have no impact whatsoever on labor supply if it simply mandates that people behave in exactly the same way that they would have behaved in the absence of the pension plan.[3] Thus, if pension contributions are perceived as substitutes for deposits that would otherwise have been made to retirement saving accounts, and pension benefits are viewed as substitutes for the benefits these accounts would otherwise have produced, the payment of contributions reduces neither the lifetime income of the household nor the net gain from working an additional hour. Any incentive to seek employment where contributions can be avoided will also disappear.

Strengthening the contribution-benefit linkage. The theory suggests that among people in the prime working ages, labor supply impacts will depend on whether the pension system is viewed as being essentially a system of forced savings or as being essentially a set of unrelated taxes and transfers. These views are likely to depend both on the way that the program appears or is portrayed and on the reality of the actual relationship between benefits and contributions.

Although they may have no impact on the actual linkage between contributions and benefits, the perception that such a linkage exists may well be affected by elements including the administrative structure employed to manage the system, the vocabulary used to describe the system, and the structure of services offered to prospective beneficiaries. For example, other things equal, a system that is managed by private sector fund managers or by an independent nonprofit organization may more effectively convey the image of a close benefit-contribution link than one managed as a government department.

The perception of a close link should also be aided by a vocabulary that employs terms such as "contributions" and "individual accounts" and that talks about benefits being "earned" as a result of contributions accumulating in the individual accounts or of a growing accumulation of pension points. Finally, where linkages exist, they will be clearer if workers receive materials that explain how benefits are calculated, and are given regular statements showing their account balances and their potential benefit entitlement. None of these necessarily changes the actual relationship between contribution payments and benefit receipts, but each can reduce labor supply impacts and increase compliance incentives by altering people's perceptions.

Even where benefits are closely linked to past contributions, whether people believe that the payment of pension contributions imposes a net burden on them will depend on whether they believe that additional contribution payments will trigger additional benefits of greater, lesser, or roughly equal value. Among the important elements that will influence this perception are the actual benefit computation rules, the implicit rate of return earned on pension contributions, and the financing mechanisms used by the plan.

The value of future benefits will most closely approximate the value of additional pension contributions where benefits are directly proportional to either earnings or contributions. The contribution-benefit linkage is loosened by features of the benefit computation that are designed to help reduce the impact on retirement benefits of contingencies such as low lifetime earnings, periods of unemployment, and child care responsibilities. Each of these features may play an important social role, but each will also tend to increase the perception that pension contributions are a net burden, particularly among those people who do not think that they will experience any of these contingencies.

Pension contributions are more likely to be viewed as a burden if the future benefits they produce imply a rate of return substantially lower than the rate that might be earned on private investments. The relationship between current contributions and future benefits will be affected by, among other things, the economic and demographic environment and the mechanisms used to finance the pensions.[4] The tax treatment of pensions and other forms of retirement savings will also play an important role.

People suffering from myopia would only save for retirement voluntarily if they received a return much higher than the rate that could be expected on private investments. Myopic people, therefore, are unlikely to consider that future benefits receipts will offset current contribution payments under any mandatory pension system.

The amount that workers actually see deducted from their pay checks usually represents only a portion of the funding of the pension system. Typically, contributions of an equal or greater amount are collected from employers, and some form of subsidy from the government's general budget is also common. Workers who assume that the only impact on their take-home pay is the deduction of their own pension contribution and who compare the deductions associated with additional work to the additional pension benefit produced by that work may conclude that the future benefits are worth more than the current contributions. If this were true, it would mean that the pension system was actually operating as a subsidy that encouraged work among younger workers.

Where labor markets are relatively free and function well, such a perception is likely to be erroneous. In those markets, the employer contribution is likely to be reflected in a lower gross wage, lowering the take-home pay of the employee in the same way that the employee contribution does.

Where labor markets do not function so well or where pensions are subsidized from the general government budget, however, the perception that the value of future benefits more than offsets the cost of current contributions may be accurate.[5] In this case, the employer contribution may actually operate as a kind of sales tax that the working-age population will have to pay even if they reduce their work effort a bit or shift out of the formal employment sector. A government subsidy financed by a value-added tax would have the same effect. Since the amount they will have to pay for pensions doesn't fall very much when they reduce work effort, there is less incentive to make such reductions.

Summary of predictions from theory. Labor supply is likely to be affected both by the amount, timing, and conditions under which benefits are paid and by the degree to which pension contributions are viewed as being linked to future benefit payments. Among the working-age population, the requirement to pay pension contributions may be viewed as imposing no particular burden if contributions are thought to trigger future benefits of equal value. Otherwise, pension contributions are likely to affect labor supply in much the same way as any other earnings tax, including discouraging work effort and creating evasion incentives.

No matter how the working-age population views contributions, however, by the time they have reached retirement age they should find that the availability of benefits constitutes an encouragement to retire. Any conditions, such as limitations on the earnings of pension recipients, that may be attached to the receipt of benefits are likely to further discourage work effort among those approaching retirement.

EMPIRICAL ANALYSES OF LABOR SUPPLY EFFECTS

The previous discussion suggests a number of important questions whose answers would provide valuable information to anyone responsible for designing a pension program and wishing to avoid unfavorable labor supply effects. Unfortunately, a number of these issues have not yet been analyzed adequately. For example, little has been done to find how perceptions are influenced by different organizational and management approaches, vocabularies, or beneficiary services, let alone how changes in perceptions might affect labor supply decisions.

The link between pension plan structure and compliance rates is often discussed, but has not been adequately researched. Informal labor markets and underground economic activity account for a major fraction of employment in some developing countries, but are hardly unknown in developed countries. Neither participants in informal labor markets nor many of the self-employed operating in the formal part of the economy have particularly good records of complying with pension contribution rules. Few studies have tried to examine the link between pension structure and compliance, however. Presumably, a closer contribution-benefit link would increase compliance incentives, but nobody knows whether it would improve compliance by a great deal or by just a little bit.[6]

The studies that address labor supply issues fall into two groups. One group examines the impact of income and employment taxes on the labor supply of working-age people. These studies tend to examine the combined impact of both pension contributions and all other taxes that depend on individual earnings. Most are not capable of detecting any differences that might exist between the two kinds of levies, even though, in theory, differences might exist.

The second group of studies examines the factors influencing retirement behavior. These studies commonly focus on the behavioral responses to changes in benefit amounts and the conditions under which benefits will be paid. They offer valuable insights about how retirement decisions can be influenced by the structure of a pension plan. They are not able to tell us, though, whether the resulting retirement patterns are closer to or farther from the patterns that could be expected in the absence of the market imperfections which pension programs were created to offset. Moreover, these studies rely overwhelmingly on the analysis of data in just a few developed countries and may not be representative of the situation in other parts of the world.

Tax impact. Studies of worker behavior typically find that among people whose work provides the main source of support for themselves and their families, employment taxes have little or no impact on work effort. Apparently, the two potential responses to a tax-related reduction in net earnings are of roughly equal force and each serves to offset the impact of the other.[7] The finding that work effort among these people is not affected substantially, however, does not necessarily rule out the possibility that high taxes have encouraged shifting of employment into sectors where taxes are lower or enforcement is weaker.

These studies also tend to find that employment taxes are likely to cause some reduction in the work effort of workers who are not the primary earners in their families or who have an alternative source of support. This would include students, married women, and people potentially eligible for social assistance benefits. Estimates of the degree of the work response vary from study to study, generally falling somewhere in the range of a reduction in hours worked of from 2 percent to 10 percent in response to a 10 percent reduction in net earnings. Although they are not huge, work-effort reductions such as these do represent a social welfare loss which must be acknowledged and weighed against the welfare gains produced by pension systems and other social welfare programs.[8]

Retirement behavior. A number of studies have attempted to understand the factors that seem most important in influencing the decisions of older workers to withdraw from the labor force.[9] This sort of behavior appears to be the product of complicated decision processes, and the data sets and technical tools needed to understand it have only recently begun to become available. Nonetheless, when taken together, the studies undertaken thus far provide some valuable information. Among the factors that fairly consistently appear to be important influences on labor force decisions are: (1) the age of the individual, (2) the availability of retirement benefits, (3) the individual's health, (4) the level of the retirement benefits to which the individual is entitled, (5) other sources of income, and (6) any earnings limitations imposed as a condition for receiving benefits.

As people get older, they are more likely to retire. While this seems obvious, the impact appears to operate independently of other influences, such as their health status and employment prospects as well as the amount of retirement income available to them. To some extent, the independent impact that age exerts may reflect the influence of social norms about when retirement is expected and when continued work is expected.

Eligibility for retirement benefits draws people out of the labor force, and the age at which benefits are first available appears to be one of the most popular ages for retirement. (The availability of benefits for invalidity or long-term unemployment has a substantial and similar impact.) In many studies, modest changes in the amount of the benefit seems to be less important than its availability.[10] The impact of first becoming eligible for benefits is even stronger in pension plans where postponing retirement after this date has little impact on future monthly benefit amounts.[11]

In principle, individuals who know they will eventually become entitled to retirement benefits could retire before they are actually able to receive those benefits, supporting themselves for a time by drawing down their personal financial assets or borrowing against their future benefit entitlement. In practice, however, this does not appear to be all that common. One possibility is that most people have insufficient assets or are not able to borrow enough to retire before the age of first eligibility for benefits. Another possibility is that the establishment of an age of first eligibility provides a social signal that many workers follow.

Declining health is commonly correlated with retirement. Most well-developed social security systems offer invalidity benefits for workers whose health has deteriorated to the point where work is no longer possible. Apparently, however, a decline in health status that is not significant enough to trigger invalidity benefits can nevertheless play an important role in encouraging retirement.

Higher benefits encourage retirement. The impact of higher benefits appears to be particularly strong among those whose health is deteriorating, so that the combination of higher benefits and deteriorating health is a particularly powerful combination encouraging retirement. The impact of benefits levels more generally seems to be relatively modest. A common proposal for dealing with the costs of an aging population is to raise the normal retirement age but allow people to continue to receive reduced benefits at earlier ages. Estimates from both the United States and Japan suggest that the reduction in benefits produced by increasing the normal retirement age by a couple of years would cause people to delay retirement by only a few months, on average.

Where private pensions play a major role in the retirement income system, their availability and generosity appear to exert an independent impact on retirement behavior. As private pension systems mature, they can become a more powerful influence on retirement behavior than the public pension system.[12]

Where countries limit the amount that people can earn and still draw a full benefit, the limit appears to provide a fairly significant work disincentive. When faced with such a test, many pensioners appear to reduce the work effort to avoid losing pension benefits.

REVIEW AND SUMMARY OF POLICY IMPLICATIONS

A careful review of what is known about the impact of public pensions on labor supply raises as many questions as it answers, but may provide some insights useful in pension policy debates.

Pension programs are created in part to deal with certain market failures. The assumption is that in the absence of a mandatory pension program, many people would not make adequate provision for their retirement. It should be expected, then, that the creation of a pension program will reduce work effort among those approaching retirement age, and the evidence suggests that pension programs do have this impact.

These programs also seem to distort some other labor supply decisions in ways that were not intended, however. While contribution changes seem to have little impact on the work effort of primary earners, they probably discourage work among secondary workers. Mandatory contributions may also create an incentive for evasion through reclassification of activities as self-employment or movement to the underground or informal economy. Presumably, tying pension benefits fairly closely to contributions will reduce the size of these disruptions, but it is not clear by how much. Moreover, nobody can say whether the kind of retirement effects currently observed are more or less than those to be expected as a consequence of removing the market imperfections, or whether the social gains from instituting a pension program justify the other labor market disruptions that it is likely to introduce.

No matter what the view may be of the appropriateness of current pension arrangements, however, they will probably have to be changed in the future. As populations age and retirees live longer, the economic cost of supporting the retired population will increase. Fiscal realities are likely to force some part of this cost increase to be offset through a combination of increases in the age of retirement or reductions in the standard of living of the retired relative to that of the working-age population.[13]

As currently structured, many public pension programs offer little incentive for continuing to work after reaching the age at which benefits are first made available. Whether this structure represents a conscious social policy adopted previously or was inadvertant, revisions to the structure which will increase the incentive to continue working are likely to prove desirable as populations continue to age.

Studies of retirement behavior suggest, however, that if those responsible for pension policy hope to induce a significant increase in the age at which people retire, they must seriously consider changing the age at which retirement benefits first become available. Apparently, taken by itself, a simple change in the amount of the benefit paid at any given retirement age is as likely to produce lower retirement incomes as it is to produce greater work effort. If officials want to get people to work longer, there may be no good alternative to increasing the age at which benefits are first payable.

Requiring people to work longer is not without its social costs, however, even when the life expectancies of retirees is generally increasing. Early retirement options in pension plans offer a degree of support for people whose health is deteriorating but is not so bad that they are eligible for invalidity benefits.

Finally, provisions which make benefit receipt conditional on having earnings less than some specified amount discourage work among those approaching retirement. Removing them is likely to increase work effort among those reaching retirement age. What is not known is whether the increase in economic activity produced by such a removal would more than offset the cost of the additional benefit payments.

Notes

1. In addition to their normal retirement provisions, pension programs have also been used to lessen the impact of changes in the structure of individual enterprises or entire economic sectors through subsidized early retirement benefits for older workers. Presumably the restructuring eventually increases social welfare even though it is accompanied by a temporary reduction in labor supply intentionally created by the provisions of the pension plan.

2. Economists call the first of these the "income effect," since it refers to the behavioral response associated with a reduction in income. They call the second the "substitution effect" since it refers to the incentive to substitute time spent out of the workplace for time spent at work when the net earnings per hour are reduced.

3. Additionally, even if it mandates behavior that would not otherwise have occurred, it will still have no impact if people are able to reverse the effect of the mandate easily. For example, the impact of a mandate that young people set aside for retirement more than they would prefer might be offset by the young people simply taking out larger home mortgage loans which they can pay off when they obtain access to the excess retirement saving.

4. These relationships are explored in chapter 7.

5. The impact of the employer's contribution on gross wages is discussed in chapter 6. If employer contributions were reflected fully in lower gross wages, social security contribution rates would have no impact on international competition. The concern over

competitiveness rests on the assumption that labor markets do not function well enough to guarantee that result.

6. Klaus Schmidt-Hebbel reports that between 1980 and 1994 (the years after the Chilean pension reform) the informal sector of the Chilean labor market shrank while the informal sector of labor markets in most of the rest of Latin America expanded. It is not possible to know, however, whether this trend represents the impact of public pension reform or of the many other economic changes occurring at the same time in Chile. See Klaus Schmidt-Hebbel, "Pension Reform, Informal Markets and Long-term Income and Welfare," paper presented at the World Bank conference, "Pension Systems: From Crisis to Reform" (Washington, D.C.: November 21–22, 1996).

7. Since these studies focus on behavior in developed, industrial economies, it is also possible that institutional barriers such as standardized hours of work per week make it more difficult for workers to make modest adjustment in work hours, even if they are interested in doing so.

8. Most of these studies are based on experience in Northern Europe and North America. For example, see *Welfare and Work Incentives, A North European Perspective*, ed. A.B. Atkinson and Gunnar Viby Morgensen (Oxford: Clarendon Press, 1993); and Robert K. Triest, "The Efficiency Cost of Increased Progressivity," ed. Joel Slemrod, *Tax Progressivity and Income Inequality* (Cambridge: Cambridge University Press, 1994), 137–69.

9. Recent reviews of this literature can be found in Michael V. Leonesio, "The Economics of Retirement: A Nontechnical Guide," *Social Security Bulletin* 59:4 (Winter 1996), 29–50; Robin L. Lumidaine, "Factors Affecting Labor Supply Decisions and Retirement Income," ed. Eric A. Hanushek and Nancy L. Maritato, *Assessing Knowledge of Retirement Behavior* (Washington, D.C.: National Academy Press, 1996), 61–122; and Kurt Magnussen, "Old-Age Pensions, Retirement Behaviour and Personal Saving," Discussion Paper PI-9609 (London: The Pensions Institute, Birbeck College, University of London, August 1996).

10. For example, Selke finds that becoming eligible for a social security pension reduces labor force participation of Japanese men by 15 percent. See Atsushi Selke, "Company Pension Plans, Public Pensions and Retirement in Japan," ed. Michael D. Hurd and Naohiro Yashiro, *The Economic Effects of Aging in the United States and Japan* (Chicago: University of Chicago Press, 1997), 295–315.

11. In OECD countries, labor force participation rates among older men are strongly correlated with the age at which public pension benefits first become available and with the impact of an additional year's work on the size of those benefits. See Jonathan Gruber and David Wise, "Social Security Progams and Retirement Around the World," *National Bureau of Economic Research*, Working Paper 6134 (August 1997).

12. Recent studies in the U.S. and the U.K. find that the people retiring earliest consist of two totally unrelated groups, those who are quite well off as a result of substantial income from private pensions and those with serious health problems. See A.B. Atkinson and Holly Sutherland, "Two Nations in Early Retirement? The Case of Britain," in A.B. Atkinson, *Incomes and the Welfare State, Essays on Britain and Europe* (Cambridge: Cambridge University Press, 1995), 95–118; and Richard V. Burkhauser, Kenneth A.

Couch and John W. Phillips, "Who Takes Early Social Security Benefits? The Economic and Health Characteristics of Early Beneficiaries," *The Gerontologist* 36:6, 789–99.

13. These issues were explored more completely in chapter 2.

Chapter Six

Public Pensions and International Competitiveness

The last several decades have seen major changes in international economic relationships. In many parts of the developed world, new competitors from abroad have entered to challenge the enterprises that have traditionally dominated domestic markets. Over time, this challenge has led to massive restructuring of key industries and economic institutions. New organizations have risen to prominence in some markets, swallowing up older enterprises or forcing them to adapt in order to survive. A new set of multinational corporations has developed a new set of global production and distribution strategies, under which production facilities are shifted from one region of the globe to another, financed by massive movements of private sector capital and leading to dramatic changes in international trade patterns. At the same time, technological change is creating a whole new set of information and service industries, together with a whole new set of prominent enterprises.

The last two decades have also witnessed a variety of macroeconomic problems in many parts of the developed world. At one time or another over this period, most of the various developed countries have seen their growth rates slow, their wage rates stagnate, and their unemployment rates rise. In combination with the changes in international economic relationships, these domestic problems have renewed interest in understanding why one economy grows more rapidly than another. These growth, trade, investment, and employment concerns are brought together in the more general concern with "international competitiveness."

In the popular press, the link between social security and international competitiveness that attracts most of the attention is the link between social security charges and employer costs. The assumption is that high social security employer contributions lead to high unit labor costs and force domestic manufacturers' prices to rise above those charged by foreign manufacturers. The fear is that this leads, in turn, to a loss of the country's export markets, an increase in the volume of imports, a movement of domestic plants abroad, lower domestic wages, and higher domestic unemployment. A closer examination of this issue reveals, however, that the interactions are much more complicated and the linkages less clear than is implied by these assumptions.

This chapter will explore some of the current thinking on the factors that influence international competitiveness and the role that might be played by social security programs. It will then discuss the relationship between pension contribution rates and employer costs and the institutional and economic conditions which might cause high pension contribution rates to undermine international competitiveness.

Social Security and International Competitiveness

What is international competitiveness? Societies differ in the rates at which they grow, develop new products, expand trade, and enrich the lives of their citizens. Although the term is rarely defined with precision, those who worry about international competitiveness seem to be concerned that a lack of competitiveness will lead initially to a decline in the number of high-wage, skilled jobs and, eventually, to declines in living standards relative to other, more competitive countries.

Economic analysis over the years finds a variety of explanations for growth and development. The concerns about the linkage between pension costs and international competitiveness seem to reflect most closely the analytical framework of the classical economists (e.g., David Ricardo) who focused on differences in endowments of land, capital, natural resources, and labor operating through the principle of comparative advantage. In the classical analysis, trade patterns reflect (among other things) the relative labor costs of different industries in different countries.

Economists later came to realize that the forces which shaped economic growth and development were much more complicated. The classical analysis implicitly assumed a static world in which products and technologies changed very slowly and growth occurred largely through the addition of more labor and more capital to the production process. Although this analysis contains many valuable insights, it is not particularly useful in explaining many of the actual international differences in rates of growth and development. Clearly, other factors are also at work.

The search for these other factors soon led to an appreciation for the role of different economic and political institutions and of a set of less measurable, more intangible influences involving social attitudes and organizations. Much economic growth in the developed world seems to be explained by rising worker skill levels, changes in technology, and improvements in the organization of both individual enterprises and the economic system. This raises a number of questions. What combinations of institutions and attitudes accounts for differences in nations' educational systems and traditions? Why do scientific breakthroughs occur one place rather than another? Why are some enterprises more effective in developing, producing, and marketing new products? Why are some economic and political systems more apt to generate such enterprises? Apparently, the determinants of international competitiveness are to be found as much in the answers to questions such as these as they are in comparisons of relative labor costs.

The International Institute for Management Development in Lausanne, Switzerland, regularly prepares a comprehensive analysis and ranking of the competitiveness of the major economies of the world. Their research has led them to conclude that international competitiveness comes from the complex interaction of a variety of different influences. Their rankings are based on over 200 measures falling into eight different categories. These include measures of the robustness of each nation's domestic economy; the quality of its basic and technological infrastructure, international trade, and financial transactions; the quality of private sector management, government fiscal policies, domestic research, and science activities; the cost of capital; and the size and quality of the workforce.[1]

The link to social security. Since the determinants of international competitiveness are not well understood, the links between social security programs and competitiveness are also unclear. There are many ways, however, in which the existence and operation of social security programs may enhance a nation's international competitiveness. An efficiently organized health system can contribute to a healthier labor force. A pension system that protects the incomes of those who become disabled and the survivors of those who die young and that reduces the need for middle-age workers to use spare economic resources to save for retirement may provide both the means and the motivation for parents to increase their investment in their children's education. Unemployment insurance and early retirement benefits can help reduce worker resistance to industrial change. In these and other ways, social security programs can help to produce the kind of behaviors and attitudes that seem to facilitate economic growth and enhance international competitiveness.

These programs can be expensive, however. Financing generous social security programs requires that a government levy high tax and/or social insurance contribution rates, which can translate into high contribution charges levied on a nation's employers. It is possible, then, that any positive impact of social security programs on international competitiveness is more than offset by the negative impact of placing a country's domestic enterprises at a cost disadvantage.

LABOR COSTS AND SOCIAL INSURANCE CONTRIBUTION RATES

Adjustments in a free market economy. The traditional analysis of the incidence of social insurance contributions in a free market economy concludes that they should not present any particular problems for international competitiveness. In this analysis, after the effects of a rate change have worked their way through the economy, employees end up bearing essentially all of the burden in the form of lower real wages. The result does not depend on how the levy is divided between the employer and the employee.[2] It means that in a free market economy, social insurance charges will have no significant impact on either employer costs or on employer demand for labor.[3]

The reason that employees are assumed to bear essentially the entire burden of social insurance contributions has to do with the degree to which the quantity of labor that workers are willing to supply in a given economy varies with the net wage they are able to earn. Anytime a tax is collected from producers according to the amount of a particular input that they use in the production process, that input's owners must accept a lower price unless they are willing to reduce the amount they sell. As a general proposition, the supply of labor is very inelastic (the quantity supplied does not change very much in response to changes in take-home pay) so that those who supply labor must accept a lower price for the work when a tax on labor is imposed. Moreover, the supply of capital is much more elastic than the supply of labor, so taxes such as social insurance contributions could not easily be shifted onto owners of capital under any circumstances. Consequently, even those workers who do end up making some adjustment in the hours they work in response to change in their net wage are going to bear virtually all of the burden of any change in pension contribution rates.

This result may be understood more easily by focusing on the various reactions that can be expected when pension contributions are imposed or their rate rises. Any change in the amount of pension contributions deducted from workers' pay simply reduces their take-home pay directly. It does not change employer costs or product costs.

The reaction of employers to an increase in their pension contribution rate is a bit more complicated. Since the rate increase causes their labor costs to increase, they will first attempt to adjust directly by simply reducing the amount of any money wage increase they would otherwise have agreed to. In this way, real wage levels net of pension contributions will gradually fall below the path they would otherwise have been on until the total cost of employing each worker falls to the level it would have occupied had contribution rates never changed.

Workers may accept the slowing of the growth in real earnings levels as a natural market phenomenon, or they may resist it. Resistance will temporarily increase the cost of labor to employers, causing them to engage in one of two kinds of actions. The more direct of the two is to reduce employment, thereby producing an increase in aggregate unemployment in the economy. Eventually, this increased unemployment serves to slow the rate of growth of money wages, achieving the necessary adjustment in net pay and encouraging employers to restore employment to previous levels.

The less direct mechanism is changes in product prices. Employers may initially recover the cost of higher pension contributions by raising product prices. Such increases cause the general price level to rise, reducing real wage levels by reducing the purchasing power of a given nominal wage. Price pressures will continue until real wages have fallen by the amount needed to offset the impact of the pension contribution increase.[4]

Impact of barriers to adjustment. The free market result need not hold, however, if government or other labor market forces are able to interfere with the adjustment process just outlined. Two potential sources of such interference are minimum wage provisions and effective anti-inflation policies.

Minimum wage levels can be established through either statute or collective bargaining. By providing a floor below which wages cannot fall, these provisions interfere with the process that would normally operate to cause the burden of pension contributions to be born by workers. In particular, if minimum wages are indexed (either formally or informally), the mandatory adjustments cannot operate to lower the real wages of workers at the minimum. These workers are protected from bearing all or a portion of the burden of the contribution increase, even though workers at higher earning levels will not be protected. The cost of employing minimum wage workers rises, forcing up unit labor costs and, most likely, leading to a reduction in the quantity of low wage workers employed.

Monetary policies (or other economic conditions) which are effective in preventing an increase in the general price level can also interfere with the adjustment process, at least for a period of time. As noted, the process through which increases in pension contributions—particularly employer contributions—are translated into lower real earnings of workers may well include a general increase in prices. Effective anti-inflationary policies can slow this adjustment process, leaving employers with higher costs for longer period of time than would otherwise be the case. The higher costs are also likely to be associated with higher unemployment.

Summary of domestic impacts. In summary, where price and wage levels are fairly free to adjust, increases in pension contributions will cause reductions in real wages, regardless of whether the increases are levied in the first instance on the employer or the employee. Where effective wage minimums prevent wages from falling and effective anti-inflation policies greatly inhibit upward adjustments in product prices, the pace at which the free market result is achieved may be slowed substantially. In the interim, both unemployment levels and unit labor costs can rise.[5]

LABOR COSTS AND INTERNATIONAL TRADE

Labor costs and flexible exchange rates. Even if adjustments in pension contribution rates caused changes in domestic labor costs, these changes would not affect international trade or the location of international manufacturing in the analysis of the classical economists. In their analysis, the rate of exchange between the currencies of two different countries was determined primarily by the relative supply and demand for the two different currencies. Supply and demand were determined, in turn, largely by trade flows. The net result was that any change in the general price level in one country sooner or later would lead to an offsetting change in that country's exchange rate. The price in another country of that country's exports would be unaffected, trade patterns would be unaffected, and manufacturing location decisions would be unaffected.

The relationships of the classical model probably still hold over the long term. Differences in domestic inflation rates and in rates of growth of labor productivity seem to be reflected in changes in the exchange rates prevailing between different currencies. But it is increasingly clear that the influence of these factors can be overshadowed during moderately long periods of time. International movements of capital into and out of particular currencies, in particular, can apparently cause exchange rates to diverge substantially from the levels that would have equalized production costs, and the reasons for these movements are not very well understood or explained.[6]

Exchange rate movements caused by international capital movements can cause manufacturing costs in one country to rise or fall relative to those in competing countries totally without regard to any underlying changes in domestic unit labor costs. Moreover, judging from recent history, the magnitude of the exchange rate movements can be sufficiently large that any impact of a change in pension contributions would be swamped by other factors, even if the change in pension contributions was translated into a change in unit labor costs.

For example, consider the relationship between the U.S. dollar and the German mark over the last 18 years. The exchange rate has varied over a range of roughly 1.7 marks to the dollar (in 1979 and again in 1997) to as high as 3.15 marks to the dollar in 1984 and as low as 1.43 marks to the dollar in 1995. If unit labor costs in manufacturing in Germany and the

United States were exactly equal in 1979 and rose at exactly the same rate in their own currencies in every year thereafter, German costs would have fallen to just over half the level of U.S. costs in the mid-1980s (yielding a significant cost advantage for Germany); risen to more than 20 percent above U.S. costs by the mid-1990s (putting Germany at a severe cost disadvantage); and returned in 1997 to approximately the same relationship they had in 1979 (making Germany and the U.S. roughly equal in their international competitiveness). Shifts of this magnitude in the international competitiveness of the two economies would have been the result solely of currency shifts. They would have had nothing to do with domestic trends in wages, productivity, or pension costs.

Labor costs when exchange rates are fixed. International cost relationships are different when countries decide to interfere in foreign exchange markets by establishing fixed exchange rates. Some form of fixed exchange rate regime has been the norm for much of recent history, taking the form of the gold standard prior to the Great Depression and the Bretton Woods system in the two decades following the Second World War. Today, many of the countries of the European Union are attempting to maintain a limited form of fixed exchange among themselves within the European Monetary Union and to create for themselves the ultimate fixed exchange system, a single currency. In other parts of the world, blocs of countries follow more or less formal policies of tying the value of their currency to that of another, particularly the French franc or the U.S. dollar.

Where exchange rates are fixed, exchange markets will not adjust automatically to offset imbalances in trade flows. Moreover, fixed exchange rates force convergence of the domestic inflation rates of participating countries. If costs in one country get out of line with those in another, the only adjustment mechanism is policies that attack the cost differentials directly.

STATISTICAL EVIDENCE

The preceding discussion suggests two possible relationships between social security and international competitiveness. Well-designed social security program expenditures can have a positive impact by enhancing educational opportunities, labor mobility, and other factors. On the other hand, where exchange rates do not respond quickly to changes in trade flows and domestic product, and labor markets are not entirely free, the cost of financing these programs can have a negative impact.

Statistical evidence drawn from the competitiveness scores of the International Institute for Management Development lends support to both possibilities, at least among OECD countries. A regression relating that organization's 1997 competitiveness score for each OECD country with the latest information on each country's total social security spending and the contribution rate levied on its employers yields the following result:

$$\text{Score} = 59.6 + 0.71 \,\%SS - 0.81 \,\text{Employer CR}$$
$$\phantom{\text{Score} =\ } (8.2) \quad\ (0.32) \quad\quad\ \ (0.25)$$
$$R^2 = 0.44$$

where "Score" is the competitiveness ranking (on a scale of 1 to 100) as calculated in 1997 by the International Institute for Management Development, "%SS" is total 1993 spending on social security programs expressed as a percent of GDP, and "Employer CR" is the 1995 employer contribution rate for all social security programs.[7]

This statistical result suggests that at the average value of each variable, a 10 percent increase in spending on social security as a percent of GDP would increase the competitiveness score by 2.5 percent, but that a similar 10 percent increase in the employer contribution rate would reduce the competitiveness score by the same amount, 2.5 percent.

SUMMARY

A variety of factors contribute to determining a country's international competitiveness. Social security spending may strengthen several of these factors, thereby enhancing a nation's competitiveness. The measures needed to finance these expenditures may have a detrimental impact on competitiveness, however, owing to their impact on relative business production costs.

Both economic theory and empirical studies suggest that where product markets, labor markets, and foreign exchange markets are allowed to operate fairly freely, pension contribution rates are unlikely to have any particular relationship with international competitiveness. Freely operating labor and product markets are likely to ensure that any increases in pension contributions are converted into lower real wage levels rather than higher business costs. The result need not hold, however, where the combination of effective anti-inflation programs and either government labor policies or private labor agreements prevent the wage adjustments needed to translate higher contributions into lower real wages. This combination can create a link between pension contributions and international competitiveness, but only where foreign exchange markets are also not entirely free.

Statistical correlations relating one set of international competitiveness scores to measures of social security spending and employer contribution rates suggest the presence of both positive influences from spending and negative influences from employer contributions. If these results are reliable indicators, both unmindful cutbacks in social security spending and an attempt to shift too much of their cost onto employers may be detrimental to international competitiveness.

NOTES

1. Stephane Garelli, "The Fundamentals of World Competitiveness," *The World Competitiveness Yearbook, 1996 Edition* (Lausanne, Switzerland: International Institute for Management Development, 1996).

2. For example, John A. Brittain, "The Incidence of Social Security Payroll Taxes," *American Economic Review* 61:1 (March 1971), 110–25; and Johnathan Gruber, "The Incidence of Payroll Taxation: Evidence from Chile," Working Paper No. 5053 (Cambridge, Mass.: National Bureau of Economic Research, 1996). Brittain looked cross-nationally at the experience of manufacturing industries. Gruber analyzed the impact of the 1981 Chilean reform in which the employer contribution was abolished and the total employer and employee contribution rate was reduced. He finds that the employees bore the entire burden both before and after the reform.

3. The result is equally applicable to the employer cost of other employee benefits financed by charges against labor compensation, not just to pension contributions.

4. Empirical studies tend to find that from one-third to one-half of the adjustment is through a slowdown in the growth of money wages and the rest is through employer changes in either the number they employ or the prices they charge. Typically, most of the adjustment occurs within one to one-and-a-half years. See Bertil Holmlund, "Payroll Taxes and Wage Inflation: The Swedish Experience," *Scandinavian Journal of Economics* 85:1 (1983), 1–15; Daniel S. Hamermesh, "New Estimates of the Incidence of the Payroll Tax," *Southern Economic Journal* (April 1979), 1208–19; or Wayne Vroman, "Employer Payroll Taxes and Money Wage Behavior," *Applied Economics* 6 (September 1974), 189–204.

5. Holmlund notes: "Labor will presumably bear the full burden of payroll tax increases in the long run, but it may take quite a while before the long run is reached." Bertil Holmlund, op cit., p. 15. In a cross-national study of eight OECD countries, Kopits found evidence of continuing factor price differentials, indicating less than full backward shifting. See George Kopits, "Factor Prices in Industrial Countries," *International Monetary Fund*, Staff Papers 29:3 (September 1982).

6. For example, Mark P. Taylor, "The Economics of Exchange Rates," *Journal of Economic Literature* 33 (March 1995), 13–47.

7. The numbers in parentheses are standard errors. The data for each country and the data sources are shown in appendix table A.

Appendix Table A

Comparison of International Scores with Social Security Spending and Employer Tax Rates, OECD Countries

Country	Score	Social Security as Percent of GDP	Employer Contribution Rate
United States	100.00	15.20	13.35
Finland	70.80	38.97	22.00
Norway	70.61	19.93	14.20
Netherlands	70.29	31.70	10.75
Switzerland	69.80	20.53	7.74
Japan	68.71	17.88	14.38
Canada	67.76	22.84	8.40
United Kingdom	67.26	21.60	10.20
Luxembourg	66.40	29.92	13.00
New Zealand	66.17	18.89	1.85
Germany	64.45	26.33	17.99
Sweden	59.56	40.05	30.96
Australia	58.59	11.75	0.00
France	58.37	24.12	34.31
Austria	57.63	25.65	25.30
Iceland	55.20	7.15	15.75
Spain	48.75	22.60	32.00
Portugal	35.12	14.84	26.75
Italy	34.67	12.40	47.62
Greece	33.14	19.79	23.90
Turkey	32.78	5.11	19.50

Source and Concepts: International competitiveness scores are from *The World Competitiveness Yearbook, 1997* (Lausanne, Switzerland: International Institute for Management Development (IMD), 1997), http://www.imd.ch/wcy/factors/overall.html. The calculation of the competitiveness index used to generate country scores was based on 220 indicators of international competitiveness. All indicators are listed and defined on IMD's web pages.

Social security as a percent of GDP data are from *The Cost of Social Security: Fifteenth International Inquiry, 1990–1993* (International Labour Office, 1997), http://www.ilo.org/public/english/110secso/css/cssindex.htm.

Employer contribution rates are from *Social Security Programs Throughout the World, 1995* (U.S. Social Security Administration, July 1995), table 3, xliii.

Chapter Seven

The Mathematics of Pension Contribution Rates

One of the more confusing aspects of the debate over the structure of public pensions involves the relationship between pension financing strategies and their associated contribution rates. This chapter focuses on various economic, demographic, and institutional factors influencing contribution rates. It begins with an analysis of an intentionally simplified world and examines the impact of introducing additional complicating factors.

The strategies used to set pension contribution rates differ on two important points: whether the calculation focuses on contributions and benefits for a group of workers or for each worker individually and whether the calculation seeks to balance income and outgo at a particular point in time or seeks balance over a period of time.

Most of the attention in this chapter will be focused on differences between the two approaches that illustrate the polar cases. One is a program of advance funded, individual savings plans which invariably follow the defined contribution approach, under which, technically, the plan specifies a contribution rate but not a pension amount. The other is a pay-as-you-go group pension plan, which is usually a defined benefit plan under which benefits are defined in relation to previous earnings.[1] Under the first approach, contribution rates are calculated so that *each worker* will contribute enough *over his or her working lifetime* to finance *his or her own* pension; the focus is the individual and the time period is the individual's lifetime. Under the second approach, contribution rates are calculated so that *workers as a group* will contribute enough *each year* to finance the aggregate amount paid that year to *pensioners as a group*; the focus is on the group and the time period is the current year.

A third approach, commonly found in occupational pension plans, is an advance funded, defined benefit, group pension plan. It mixes features of the other two approaches in that benefits are defined but assets that can be used to finance the pensions are accumulated in advance. The calculation of contribution rates under the third approach is more complicated than under the other two. Essentially, however, the starting point is determining what *workers as a group* would have to contribute *over the lifetime of the group* to finance *the group's own* pensions. This result is often then adjusted to spread the fiscal impact of one-time or unexpected developments over several cohorts. With just a few exceptions that will be noted, the factors influencing contribution rates affect this third approach in the same way that they affect the individual savings approach.

THE SIMPLE MODEL

The easiest place to begin is with a simple example employing the following key characteristics:

(1) Workers enter the labor market on their 22nd birthday, work full time for the next 43 years, and retire on their 65th birthday.

(2) Once retired, individuals receive an annual pension, live another 17 years, and all die on their 82nd birthday.

(3) Each worker earns the same wage as every other worker (regardless of age) in any given year.

(4) Pensions are set at a level that will replace one-half of the worker's average lifetime wage and are updated after retirement to reflect changes in prevailing wage levels.

(5) Pensions are financed entirely through contributions (and, where applicable, interest earnings).

(6) Either price levels never change or they change at a constant rate that is fully reflected in both the rate of increase of wages and the interest rate.[2]

To start with the simplest of all possible worlds, also assume that: (1) wage levels do not change, (2) the interest rate is zero, and (3) the population is constant (the number of people born into this society each year has been and always will be the same as the number reaching age 82 and dying). Focus now on how pensions can be financed in this simple world.

The individual savings option involves requiring each worker to save a given portion of his or her earnings each year, with the amount to be set aside calculated so that at retirement it provides a stock of assets just large enough to finance the pension for the rest of the worker's life. Since the initial example assumes a zero interest rate and no wage growth, it is easy to calculate what each worker will have to set aside. Each will need to have at retirement a balance equal to 8.5 times the average wage, from which he or she can withdraw 0.5 times the average wage for each of the 17 years in retirement. To accumulate such a fund during 43 working years requires annual contributions of 19.8 percent (the balance, 8.5, divided by the years, 43) of the average wage.

A system based on this kind of advanced savings will not reach full maturity for a number of years; in this example, it is 60 years before the workers of the first cohort have spent their entire lifetimes under the system. Once the system reaches maturity, however, the simple system outlined here can continue to function indefinitely in a completely balanced manner.[3]

Although somewhat more cumbersome than the calculations made thus far, it is also possible to compute the amount of financial assets that are accumulated in this process by adding up the amounts in each worker's and retiree's account. In this particular case, the average balance in the accounts of all workers and retirees is a sum equal to just over four times the average wage.

In this very simple example, the financial requirements under the pay-as-you-go approach are just as easy to understand. Under this second approach, the amount each worker is required to contribute is calculated as the amount required to produce enough revenue to pay the pensions to the retired population. Using the assumption of 1,000 births a year, the calculation simply requires that the aggregate amount of the annual pensions (8,500 times the average wage) be divided by the aggregate amount of the workers' earnings (43,000 times the average wage). The result is a contribution rate of 19.8 percent, the same as the rate required under the mandatory retirement savings approach.

Although the contribution rates are the same in this example, the approaches differ in important ways. Under the pay-as-you-go approach, soon after the plan is started, full pensions can be paid either to newly retired workers or to the entire aged population. But the corollary is that no financial assets are accumulated during the start-up phase of the plan. In contrast, as the individual account system is maturing it creates a substantial stock of financial assets. Subsequent pensions are financed by trading this pool of assets among workers and retirees.

THE IMPACT OF ECONOMIC AND DEMOGRAPHIC VARIATIONS

Changes in certain economic and demographic assumptions cause dramatic changes in the contributions required under the two different approaches. Contribution rates under pay-as-you-go pension arrangements are quite sensitive to changes in the birth rate, but are not sensitive to changes in either the rate of growth of wages or in interest rates (as long as benefits are continually updated to reflect prevailing wage levels). In contrast, contribution rates under individual savings approaches are quite sensitive to changes in either interest or wage growth rates, but not to changes in the birth rate.

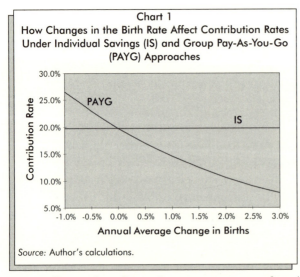

Chart 1
How Changes in the Birth Rate Affect Contribution Rates Under Individual Savings (IS) and Group Pay-As-You-Go (PAYG) Approaches

Source: Author's calculations.

These linkages can be illustrated by varying one or more of the assumptions incorporated in the simple model and tracing the impact on contribution rates. The results of these kinds of simulations are illustrated in charts 1 through 3 (and shown in appendix table A).

Changes in the birth rate alter the ratio of retirees to workers, changing the contribution rate required to finance benefits under a pay-as-you-go plan. An increase in the birth rate increases the number of new workers entering the labor force each year relative to the number reaching retirement age. Since a larger fraction of the total population is young, the contribution required to finance a given level of retirement benefits is proportionately smaller. Pensions in the simple model outlined above require contribution rates as high as 23 percent if the number of births (and hence the total population) each year declines at a constant rate of 0.5 percent per year. Contributions fall as low as 9 percent if the number of births (and hence the total population) grows at an average rate of 2.5 percent per year.

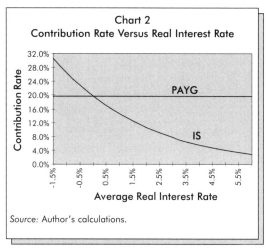

Chart 2
Contribution Rate Versus Real Interest Rate

Source: Author's calculations.

Under a pay-as-you-go approach, declining population growth rates translate directly into higher contribution rates. Birth rates have no direct effect on the contribution needed under a defined contribution, individual savings plan or under an advance funded occupational pension plan.

Changes in the interest rate have a dramatic effect on the required contribution under the savings approach. Higher interest rates increase the speed with which previous contributions placed in the worker's account grow and also reduce the target amount that the worker must accumulate, since interest earned after retirement will finance a part of the pension cost. Both phenomena mean that higher interest rates allow for lower contribution rates. Modifying our simple model to incorporate the effect of different interest rates illustrates the power of compound interest over a 43-year working life and 17-year retirement. At an

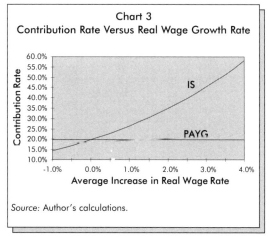

Chart 3
Contribution Rate Versus Real Wage Growth Rate

Source: Author's calculations.

interest rate of 5 percent, the required contribution falls from almost 20 percent to just under 4 percent.[4]

One side effect of the lower required contribution is that the average balance in the individual accounts (and the total volume of financial assets accumulated during the start-up phase) is smaller. At a 5 percent interest rate, the average worker in our simple example accumulates only 5.6 times the average wage in order to finance the same pension amount that required 8.5 times the average wage when the interest rate was zero. The total accumulated in all accounts is also proportionately smaller.

Changes in the rate of growth of wages are just as powerful, but have the opposite effect. If pensions are to be tied to average lifetime wages, a wage increase today means a pension increase in retirement. In the pay-as-you-go system outlined here, a general increase in everyone's wage will cause an equal percentage change in both the pensions of retirees and the wages of the contributors, leaving the required contribution rate unchanged.[5] When the higher pension must be paid from accumulated savings, however, the effect of the wage increase can be offset only by increasing the required contribution rate. In the example outlined here, if wages grow at 3 percent per year but the interest rate remains zero, the contribution rate would rise to 45 percent.

The contribution rate required under the individual savings approach can be thought of as controlled not so much by the independent effects of wage growth rates and interest rates as by the interaction of the two. In fact, as is illustrated in chart 4, the necessary contribution rate is determined, essentially, by the difference between the wage rate and the interest rate. Whenever the interest rate is 2 percent higher than the rate of growth of wages, the required contribution is 10.6 percent; when the gap is 1 percent,

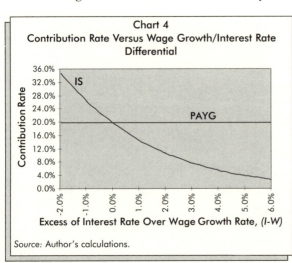

Chart 4
Contribution Rate Versus Wage Growth/Interest Rate Differential

Excess of Interest Rate Over Wage Growth Rate, (I-W)

Source: Author's calculations.

the contribution rate rises to about 14.6 percent; when the two are equal, the contribution rises to 19.8 percent; and so forth.[6]

In the analysis presented thus far, the contribution rates for an advance funded, group occupational pension plan would be the same as those for the individual savings approach.

CONTRIBUTION RATE COMPARISONS IN THE SIMPLE MODEL

Pay-as-you-go contribution rates can be either above or below the contribution rates required in the individual savings approach, depending on the particular combination of birth rates, wage growth rates, and interest rates. Rates under the two approaches will be the same only when the three relate in a particular way. In the simplified model, equality occurs when the rate of growth of births is the same as the amount by which the interest rate exceeds the wage growth rate.[7]

The interaction of these different economic and demographic variables is illustrated in chart 5. The horizontal axis of chart 5 traces different values of the amount by which the interest rate could exceed the wage growth rate. To the right of zero, the interest rate is higher than the wage growth rate; to the left of zero, wages grow faster than the interest rate. The vertical axis traces different rates of growth in annual births (and, therefore, in the total population—at least in the simple model). The area above zero represents a growing population while the area below zero represents population decline.

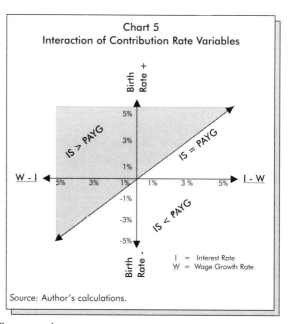

Chart 5
Interaction of Contribution Rate Variables

I = Interest Rate
W = Wage Growth Rate

Source: Author's calculations.

Chart 5 is divided by a diagonal line that represents the combinations of population growth, wage growth, and interest rates under which contribution rates are the same under the two approaches. Under economic and demographic situations that lie above (or to the left) of the line, a pay-as-you-go pension plan will have a lower contribution rate. Under situations that lie below (or to the right) of the line, the individual savings approach (or any other kind of advance funded group plan) has the lower contribution rate. The farther one moves from the line, the greater is the difference between the two systems' contribution rates.

Over the last three decades, birth rates have fallen in all developed countries and in many developing countries. Wage growth in most OECD countries has slowed substantially and real rates of return on investment have risen in the last two decades. Each of these trends has the effect of moving societies downward and to the right on chart 5. If they continue in the future, they will have the effect of increasing the pay-as-you-go contribution rate relative to the contribution rate required under advance funded plans. These economic and demographic developments provide a part of the explanation for increased interest in making greater use of the advance funded approaches to financing pensions.

MORE REALISTIC ADMINISTRATIVE AND DEMOGRAPHIC ASSUMPTIONS

Clearly, substantial differences exist between the characteristics of the model discussed thus far and the real world. One major category of differences involves the impact of an uncertain and constantly changing economic and demographic environment. The analysis in this chapter compares the long-term impacts of different constant environments. In contrast, real world economies are constantly in transition, and the patterns of these transitions can be more important than the exact characteristics of a destination that will never be reached. The implications of irregular and unpredictable changes in demographic and economic values are explored in later chapters.[8]

Another major category involves more realistic treatment of mortality patterns and administrative arrangements. This second category needs to be explored briefly here because the omission of these factors alters the relationship between the various pension financing approaches, causing individual savings approaches to appear more favorable relative to pay-as-you-go approaches.

Mortality. Simulations presented thus far assume no mortality prior to retirement age, an assumption that hides a significant difference between the individual savings and group pension approaches. In individual savings plans, assets accumulated in a worker's account become a part of the worker's estate at the time of the worker's death, whether the death occurs before or after the worker retires. In contrast, group pension plans may or may not award residual benefit rights to workers dying before they retire. Any benefit rights lost due to preretirement deaths are reprogrammed into reductions in the contribution rate required to finance the benefits of those who survive.[9]

The quantitative importance of this difference will depend on the actual vesting policies and particular pattern of mortality rates found in a given society. To gain an appreciation of the possible magnitude of this effect, the simple model presented earlier was altered to employ a life table with a more realistic pattern of age-specific mortality rates. This table implies a life expectancy at age 65 of 17 years, essentially the same as the assumption employed earlier. The more realistic mortality pattern reduces the pay-as-you-go contribution rate by about 10 percent, from 19.8 percent to 17.4 percent.[10]

Administrative expenses. Pension system administrative expenses vary widely from one country to another and from one institution to another within a particular country, making generalizations somewhat risky. Nevertheless, the evidence does suggest that a decentralized system of individual financial accounts is more expensive to administer than is a large, group pension plan and that pensions which must manage investment portfolios are more expensive to administer than those that do not.

Administrative costs are the lowest under a mature pay-as-you-go, public retirement system. For example, total administrative costs account for only about 0.6 percent of total expenditures in the public pension system of the United States. Apparently, that figure is fairly representative of administrative costs in the OECD in general, but that, expressed as a percentage of contributions, administrative costs are systematically lower in the OECD countries than in developing countries.[11]

The administrative costs of advance funded pension institutions are more commonly expressed as a ratio to assets managed rather than as a percentage of either contributions or expenditures. Studies suggest that costs in large United States defined benefit pension plans average about 0.5 percent of the assets under management.[12] Administrative costs of this magnitude have the same impact on required contribution rates as does reducing the interest rate by 0.5 percentage points.

The highest administrative costs are those associated with the individual savings account approach. In the United Kingdom, the Government Actuary estimates that typical charges for administering personal pensions are 8 percent of contributions, plus 0.9 percent of assets being managed.[13] Administrative expenses in the Chilean pension funds average around 1.7 percent of assets, a charge which will produce a slightly higher total than was estimated for the United Kingdom.[14]

Cost of individual annuities. Pay-as-you-go pension programs almost always pay benefits in the form of life annuities, and advance funded group pension plans usually do (though traditions vary from country to country). The practice varies in individual savings plans. Holders of personal pensions in the United Kingdom are required to annuitize at least part of their assets. In contrast, the individual systems being constructed in Latin America tend not to require that benefits be taken as life annuities, although they may offer an annuity option. As will be discussed more fully in chapter 10, when the purchase of annuities is not required, sellers of individual annuities must charge more than an annuity would cost if it simply reflected prevailing market interest rates and current mortality experience for the population as a whole. In that situation, the difference between the pure annuity figure and the amount an individual pays on the single premium annuity market may be as much as 25 percent.

Adjusting the simple model results. Table 1 and chart 6 show the effect that plausible adjustments for each of these effects might have on the contribution rates required under the different approaches. For these purposes, pay-as-you-go pension system administrative costs were assumed to amount to 2 percent of contributions, or some three times as high as the actual figure for the United States. In these calculations, administrative costs of advance funded group plans are assumed to be 0.5 percent of assets and costs of individual account approaches are assumed to be 8 percent of contributions and 0.9 percent of assets, the average applicable to the United Kingdom's experience. Individual annuities purchased under the individual savings approach were assumed to cost 15 percent of the total amount of assets annuitized.

When taken together, the adjustments discussed in this section have a measurable impact on some of the contribution rate differences seen in the simple model. For example, data in table 1 show that in the simple model, the contribution rate under the individual savings approach was just a little over half the level required under the pay-as-you-go approach when the interest rate exceeded the wage growth rate by 2 percent and the population was constant. The effect of these three adjustments is to more than eliminate the difference between the individual savings approach and the pay-as-you-go approach and to open up a significant difference between the contribution rate required under group pension plans and the rate required under the individual accounts approach.[15]

Table 1
Adjusting Contribution Rates for Realistic Mortality Assumptions, Program Administrative Expenses, and Adverse Selection Costs

Interest Rate	0.0%	1.0%	2.0%
Base Scenario			
PAYG	19.77%	19.77%	19.77%
IS	19.77%	14.57%	10.64%
Advance GP	19.77%	14.57%	10.64%
Above Plus Administrative Costs			
(2% of contribution for PAYG; 8% of contributions + 0.9% of assets for IS; 0.5% of assets for advance funded group plan)			
PAYG	20.17%	20.17%	20.17%
IS	28.03%	20.85%	15.36%
Advance GP	22.94%	16.99%	12.47%
Above Plus Annuity Fee			
(15% of assets for IS only; 0% for PAYG, advance funded group plan)			
PAYG	20.17%	20.17%	20.17%
IS	32.98%	24.53%	18.06%
Advance GP	22.94%	16.99%	12.47%
Above Plus Early Mortality			
(Uses U.S. life table for males born in 1960)			
PAYG	17.80%	17.80%	17.80%
IS	32.98%	24.53%	18.06%
Advance GP	*	*	*

Assumptions: Birth rate is constant; wage growth = 0
Source: Author's calculations.
*Depends on how plan treats preretirement death
Note: The base scenario assumes that all workers enter the labor force at age 22, work exactly 43 years, retire on their 65th birthday, and die exactly 17 years later on their 82nd birthday. While working, each earns the average wage. In retirement, each receives a benefit equal to one-half the average wage (indexed to average wage levels). The calculations assume that all payments are made once a year on the final day of the year. PAYG denotes the contribution rate required under a pay-as-you-go, defined benefit pension plan; IS denotes this for advance funded, individual savings plans; and Advance GP denotes this for advance funded (defined benefit), group plans.
The second set of calculations incorporates all of the assumptions outlined above except that the contribution calculations are adjusted to show the gross contribution needed to pay a benefit of 50 percent of average wages and also cover the administrative costs associated with each plan. The cost assumptions are shown in the table.
The third set is a recalculation of the second set using a real life table (U.S. males born in 1960). The sample life table used previously assumed all retirees lived through retirement and died at age 82. In using the real life table, some workers will die prior to retirement. This lowers the pay-as-you-go contribution rate 2.4 percent from the preceding example.

INCREASED LONGEVITY

Populations are aging in most of the countries of the world because of the simultaneous impact of two different demographic trends, declining birth rates and longer life spans. As noted previously, changes in birth rates have a significant impact on the contribution rate required under a pay-as-you-go pension plan but do not have a direct impact on the contribution rate under advance funded approaches. In contrast, changes in life expectancy have much more similar impacts on the two approaches to pension financing.

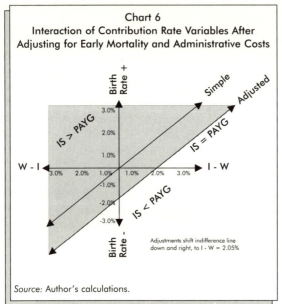

Chart 6
Interaction of Contribution Rate Variables After Adjusting for Early Mortality and Administrative Costs

Adjustments shift indifference line down and right, to I - W = 2.05%

Source: Author's calculations.

In the simple case set forth at the beginning of this brief, changes in life expectancy have exactly the same impact on contribution rates. Consider, for example, the impact of an increase from 17 to 20 in the number of years that all workers live after retirement. Under the pay-as-you-go approach and a constant population, the number of retirees will increase from 17,000 to 20,000, the number of workers will remain constant, and the required contribution rate will rise from 19.8 percent to 23.3 percent. Likewise, under the individual account approach, each worker will have to save enough to support himself for 20 years rather than 17 years. When the interest rate is zero and wages are constant, this will force the worker to increase his contributions from 19.8 percent of his pay to 23.3 percent.

Appendix table B shows a number of examples of the impact of this change in life expectancy in the context of the original model. Basically, the contribution rates rise under both approaches by roughly the same percentage. However, contribution rates under each approach become somewhat more sensitive to variations in the economic and demographic environment as the lifespan in retirement lengthens. The effect is more muted in the pay-as-you-go approach than in the individual savings approach.

Summary

This chapter focuses on the interaction between demographic and economic conditions and pension contribution rates. The analysis employs highly simplified examples to illustrate the relationships. Although the values employed are plausible, the results are not necessarily applicable to any particular country or situation. Nevertheless, the exercise does appear to justify several generalizations about contribution rates under the two systems.

The contribution rates required for producing a given retirement pension are sensitive to both economic and demographic conditions, but in different ways. Pay-as-you-go systems are sensitive to changes in birth rates but are insensitive to changes in prevailing interest rates and (when benefits are linked to wages) to the rate of growth of wages.[16] Advance funded approaches are the opposite, being sensitive to changes in the rate of growth of wages and interest rates but not to changes in the birth rate. Contribution rates under the different approaches are equally sensitive to changes in post-retirement mortality rates.

Depending on the particular demographic conditions prevailing in a given society at a given time, individual savings contribution rates may either be higher or lower than pay-as-you-go rates. Two changes that have affected much of the developed world over at least the last several decades, declines in birth rates and stagnating wage levels, have had the impact of lowering the contribution rate for individual savings plans relative to the pay-as-you-go rate.

Under any of these simulations, the pay-as-you-go rate reflects the actual volume of pension payments. Contribution rates under individual savings approaches can be either higher or lower because the individual approach has both a second source of income (interest earnings) and a second use for contributions (to keep account balances up to date with prevailing wage levels). It is the interaction of these alternative sources and uses of retirement funds that determines the relationship of the contribution rates under the two approaches.

Administrative costs and pooling the risks of preretirement mortality reduce the contribution rates required under either of the group approaches relative to those of the individual savings approach, and probably by more under pay-as-you-go plans than under private group plans. These impacts will depend on particular structures and policies, however, and may be more important in some countries' approaches than in others.

Notes

1. For the purpose of this chapter, the PAYG plan could also be what has been called a "notional defined contribution plan" under which benefits are based on accumulated contributions but the contributions earn interest at the rate that wages grow, rather than at market interest rates.

2. Chapter 10 considers the impact on pensions when prices change in ways that are not anticipated and not reflected in interest rates.

3. For example, if there are 1,000 births each year, the population at each age level will be 1,000. This means there will be 43,000 workers (1,000 each at the 43 ages from 22 to 64) and 17,000 retirees (1,000 each at the 17 ages from 65 to 81). As a group, the retirees will be supporting themselves by selling each year assets amounting to 8,500 times the average wage (17,000 retirees each financing a pension of 0.5 times the average wage). As a group, each year the workers will be buying assets equal to 8,500 times the average wage (43,000 workers setting aside 19.8% of their wage). The pensions are being financed entirely through the transfer of assets from the retirees to the workers, and the volume of assets being sold each year by retirees exactly matches the volume being purchased by workers.

4. For simplicity, in these and other similar calculations underlying this chapter, it is assumed that all wages are earned and all contributions, benefits, and interest are paid on the last day of the year. Thus, interest earnings reflect the previous year's ending balance before any contributions are added or benefits are deducted. Calculations based on monthly or weekly payments would produce slightly different numbers but not affect any of the important results.

5. If benefits after retirement were indexed to prices rather than wages, both the pay-as-you-go and individual savings systems would be sensitive to changes in wage patterns that were not reflected equally in changes in prices.

6. In this discussion, a gap between wage growth rates and interest rates is defined as the percentage amount by which one exceeds the other. For example, if the interest rate (i) is 2 percent more than the rate of growth of wages (w), then $(1+i)$ is equal to $(1+w)$ times 1.02, or, put differently, the ratio of the two, $(1+i)/(1+w)$, is equal to 1.02.

7. This mathematical result merely confirms the insight to be gained by focusing on how fast the resources available to pay pensions are growing under each of the two financing approaches. Under a pay-as-you-go system, a constant contribution rate will generate

revenues that grow each year at the rate that the working-age population is growing plus the rate at which average wages are growing. Since the future pension to be paid to each worker is also growing at the same rate as wages are growing, if the population is growing at 1 percent per year the system as a whole generates revenues per worker that grow 1 percent per year faster than the pension liability. Similarly, under the advance funding approach, contributions must earn a rate of return at least equal to the rate at which wages are growing in order to assure that future pensions can rise in line with future wages. When the interest rate exceeds this amount by 1 percent, the revenues available to finance each worker's pension grow at 1 percent per year faster than the pension liability. Since we assume that the resources available for financing each worker's pension are growing at the same rate under each of the two pension financing approaches, the required contribution rate is also the same under each of the approaches. For a more technical analysis of all of these relationships, see Henry J. Aaron, "The Social Insurance Paradox," *Canadian Journal of Economics* 32 (August 1966).

8. The implication of changing economic and demographic environments during a working career is considered in chapter 9. The implications of inflation after retirement are considered in chapter 10.

9. Both individual and group pension plans have mechanisms for helping to support the survivors of deceased workers, but these are often operated as separate aspects of the respective programs.

10. The particular life table used in this example is the table for United States males born in 1960 (turning age 65 in the year 2025) as estimated by the actuaries of the U.S. Social Security Administration. See U.S. Social Security Administration, *Life Tables for the United States Social Security Area, 1980-2080*, Actuarial Study No. 107 (August 1992). The life expectancy doesn't match the base case perfectly, so the individual savings contribution rate actually drifted up a little.

11. The U.S. figure is from the *1996 Annual Report of the Board of Trustees of the Federal Old-Age and Survivors Insurance and Disability Insurance Trust Funds*, (Washington, D.C.: Government Printing Office, 1996). For a comparison of administrative costs in different country's systems, see Olivia S. Mitchell, "Administrative Costs in Public and Private Retirement Systems," Working Paper 96-4 (Philadelphia, Penn.: The Pension Research Council of the Wharton School of the University of Pennsylvania, 1996), table 1. Unfortunately, the comparisons are hampered by the inclusion of health expenditures in some of the cases (including that of the United States). Data from the World Bank suggest that administrative costs are even lower in the public pension system in Japan and are not much higher in the Swiss system. See The World Bank, *Averting the Old-Age Crisis* (1994), 312.

12. Ibid.

13. Plus a flat charge of £2.50 per month. See "Occupational and Personal Pension Schemes: Review of Certain Contracting-Out Terms." Presented to Parliament by the Secretary of State for Social Security, March 1996.

14. These estimates are also consistent with estimates of the administrative costs of employer-sponsored, individual savings plans (called 401(k) plans) in the United States,

under which fund management fees average 1.4 percent of assets. This does not include costs incurred by the employer in operating these plans. See Olivia Mitchell, loc. cit. Apparently, these estimates also ignore the additional costs associated with trading securities. In the United States, securities trades for institutional traders typically involve fees averaging some 0.5 percent of the transaction price. See Dean Baker, "Saving Social Security with Stocks: The Promises Don't Add Up" (New York: The Twentieth Century Fund, 1997).

15. No attempt was made to simulate the impact of preretirement mortality on private defined benefit plans owing to the wide variation in the provisions of these plans in this situation. In addition to their impact on the contribution rates, the adjustments introduced here also recognize that the three approaches to producing retirement incomes also differ in other important characteristics. Individual account approaches cost more because they produce estates for those who die early and may offer the option of not taking one's retirement income in the form of a life annuity. Each may serve a worthwhile social purpose, but each also raises the contribution rate needed to generate a given pension amount. Also, at least a part of their higher administrative costs may reflect a higher quality of service to program participants.

16. Where benefits are linked to price growth rather than wage growth, changes in the rate of growth of real wages would have in a system paying price-indexed benefits.

APPENDIX TABLE A

Contribution Rates for Pay-As-You-Go (PAYG) and Individual Savings (IS) Approaches under Different Economic and Demographic Rate Assumptions

Interest Rate	0.0%	0.0%	2.0%	3.0%	3.0%	3.0%	5.0%
Wage Increase	0.0%	2.0%	3.0%	0.0%	1.0%	3.0%	3.0%
Birth Growth Rate = -0.5%							
PAYG	22.94	22.94	22.94	22.94	22.94	22.94	22.94
IS	19.77	34.91	26.33	7.70	10.71	19.77	10.84
Birth Growth Rate = -0.0%							
PAYG	19.77	19.77	19.77	19.77	19.77	19.77	19.77
IS	19.77	34.91	26.33	7.70	10.71	19.77	10.84
Birth Growth Rate = 0.5%							
PAYG	16.99	16.99	16.99	16.99	16.99	16.99	16.99
IS	19.77	34.91	26.33	7.70	10.71	19.77	10.84
Birth Growth Rate = 1.0%							
PAYG	14.57	14.57	14.57	14.57	14.57	14.57	14.57
IS	19.77	34.91	26.33	7.70	10.71	19.77	10.84

Source: Author's calculations.

APPENDIX TABLE B

The Impact of Changes in Post-Retirement Mortality on Contribution Rates under Pay-As-You-Go (PAYG) and Individual Savings (IS) Approaches

Interest Rate	0.0%	0.0%	2.0%	3.0%	3.0%	3.0%	5.0%
Wage Increase	0.0%	2.0%	3.0%	0.0%	1.0%	3.0%	3.0%
If Retirees Live for...	**The Contribution Will Be...**						
Pay-As-You-Go							
17 Years	19.77	19.77	19.77	19.77	19.77	19.77	19.77
20 Years	23.26	23.26	23.26	23.26	23.26	23.26	23.26
Individual Savings							
17 Years	19.77	34.91	26.33	7.70	10.71	19.77	10.84
20 Years	23.26	42.39	31.44	8.7	12.25	23.26	12.41

Source: Author's calculations.

Chapter Eight

Choices of Pension Approaches and Transitions Between Approaches

The debate over the structure of social security pensions involves concerns about both the most desirable structure for the long term and the issues involved in transitions from one approach to another. This chapter looks more closely at the issues involved in selecting an initial approach and in deciding to change from a pay-as-you-go to an advance funded approach.

SELECTING AMONG THE BASIC APPROACHES

Pension options. Public retirement programs tend to follow one of three basic approaches, although these approaches can be implemented through a variety of different institutional arrangements.

One approach involves *universal pension programs*, which offer essentially the same benefit to all aged residents without regard to any previous employment or the value of any prior pension contributions. In some countries benefits under such programs are adjusted to reflect other sources of income for each individual, while in other countries benefits are paid without regard to income levels.

Another approach involves *contributory defined benefit pension plans*, offering pensions only to those who previously worked under the pension plan for at least a minimum amount of time and paying benefits that reflect some combination of average preretirement earnings levels and years spent in employment covered by the plan. These pension plans can be operated either by the government or by nongovernmental organizations, may be either pay-as-you-go or advance funded, and vary widely in the strength of the linkage between the size of prior contributions and the amount of retirement benefits.

A third approach involves *defined contribution* approaches which can either be operated by financial institutions on behalf of individual workers or be sponsored by employers.[1] Under these plans, benefits at retirement reflect the amount of prior contributions to the plan and the investment returns earned by those contributions.

Pension program objectives. Selections from this menu of options will reflect each society's unique cultural traditions and social philosophies, its stage of development and economic needs, and the relative importance it attaches to achieving different public policy objectives. Different societies will make different decisions, in large part due to differences in:

(1) social attitudes about the relative importance of group cohesiveness and individual choice, the desirability of a close linkage between current benefits and prior contributions, and the acceptability of applying income testing procedures to a large fraction of the population;

(2) views about the desirable pace for phasing in both pension benefits and the associated mechanisms for raising the required revenues, whether from worker and/or employer contributions, the general budget, or other private sector sources;

(3) opinions about the wisdom and potential value of using pension institutions to achieve other social goals, particularly assembling resources for infrastructure investment, increasing national saving rates, or fostering the development of sophisticated financial markets;

(4) assessments of the likely relationship between pension arrangements and future tax or contribution rates, in particular whether advance funded pensions are likely to involve lower taxes or contributions; and

(5) the relative level of trust the population is willing to place in government on the one hand and private financial market institutions on the other.

Initial decisions are more likely to reflect social philosophy, practical issues involving the pace of implementation, and, in some cases, the need to assemble resources for infrastructure investment. Some years later, these decisions may be revisited either because of changes in philosophy or because of greater weight given to other potential concerns.

STARTING A NEW PENSION PROGRAM

The three generic approaches to retirement programs differ substantially in the speed at which pensions are phased in for the retired population and the pace at which contribution rates rise to their ultimate level. chart 1 illustrates these differences.[2]

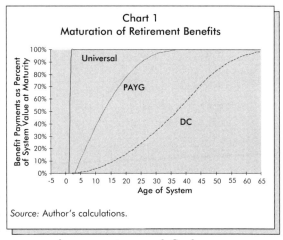

Chart 1
Maturation of Retirement Benefits

Source: Author's calculations.

Under a universal approach, full benefit payments to all individuals over the statutory retirement age can begin as soon as the system is started. Such a system matures instantly—all retirees receive full benefits as soon as the system is instituted. The tax rate required to finance the system also jumps immediately to its ultimate level.

Benefits under a contributory, pay-as-you-go system mature more slowly.[3] Those who are retired at the time the pension plan begins are not eligible for benefits, but newly retiring workers are usually allowed full credit for previous employment without regard to whether such employment was before or after initiation of the pension system. The result is that pension payments begin shortly after the system is inaugurated and rise steadily thereafter. Under the assumptions used to construct chart 1, payments reach half of their ultimate level about 13 years after the system is started and 90 percent of the ultimate level some 26 years after the system begins. If benefits are financed on a pay-as-you-go basis, contribution rates will rise to their ultimate level at the same pace as benefit payments mature.

Under the defined contribution, individual savings approach, contributions are set at their ultimate level as soon as (or relatively soon after) the plan is started, but pension payments mature quite slowly. Benefits are paid only to those making contributions before retirement and no credit is given for service prior to the date the pension system began. Cohorts retiring in the first few years after the system is initiated receive pensions, but the amount is quite small owing to the short period of time over which contributions were made.

Payments under the individual savings approach are not likely to reach half of their ultimate level until a quarter-century or more after the program is started. By then, over 90 percent of the aged population would be receiving some benefit, but none of them would have had a chance to work long enough under the program to become entitled to a full benefit. Aggregate benefit payments to the retired population are not likely to reach 90 percent of their ultimate value for at least half a century.

The substantial delay between the imposition of contributions and the emergence of adequate benefits is a serious disadvantage of the defined contribution approach, but it allows the pension system to accumulate a substantial volume of financial assets during the start-up phase, as illustrated in chart 2. The pace of asset accumulation will depend on the economic environment and the generosity of the pensions being financed. In the initial years, most of the assets are accumulating in accounts held by workers. As the system matures so that an increasing fraction of workers have spent their entire work career under the program, the aggregate amount of assets in worker accounts stops growing. Later, as increasing numbers of retirees have also spent their entire career under the system, aggregate assets held by retirees also stop growing. But the accumulation phase of the system

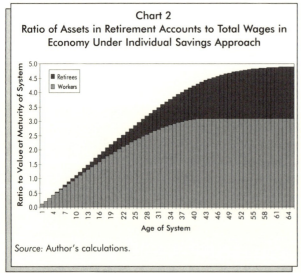

Chart 2
Ratio of Assets in Retirement Accounts to Total Wages in Economy Under Individual Savings Approach

Source: Author's calculations.

lasts for the entire half-century or more required for aggregate payments to the retired population to reach their full potential.[4]

The simulations represented in charts 1 and 2 illustrate the fiscal dilemmas with which the designers of a new pension system must struggle. A noncontributory approach can deal with retiree income problems immediately, although contributions (or general tax rates) must be imposed simultaneously at the rate implied by a fully mature system. Noncontributory benefits are often set at lower levels than are benefits under contributory programs, however, somewhat mitigating the impact of the sudden imposition of the required new revenue source.

Neither of the contributory approaches is effective in dealing with the income needs of those who are now elderly. The typical pay-as-you-go scheme can be phased in rapidly enough to address the income needs of those approaching retirement at the time the plan begins, but the individual account approach will not be sufficient by itself for any but the workers who are youngest when the system starts. In contrast, at least at the outset, contribution rates are likely to be higher under the individual accounts approach, due to the need for asset accumulation in the individual accounts.

Evolution to Mixed Approaches

Given the wide range of options and the variation in both economic conditions and cultural and social traditions, it is not surprising that the initial systems adopted around the world exhibited a fair degree of diversity. Some countries started with systems that relied mainly on universal, noncontributory pensions (usually, but not universally, paid without an income test). Others started with contributory group pensions similar to the current pay-as-you-go models, perhaps supplemented by an income-tested universal pension intended as a temporary program for those who retired before the contributory system matured. Still others began with centrally managed systems of individual savings accounts.

Over time, these approaches have been modified in a variety of ways in response to changing economic and social conditions. In the process, the systems in many countries have evolved to include a mixture of public and private management and of pay-as-you-go and advance funded elements.

Major differences remain, however, in the relative importance of the different elements of the mixture and the composition of the elements in which participation is mandatory.

One step in the evolutionary process has been the gradual shift in many publicly managed plans from some degree of advance funding to pay-as-you-go financing. It was not uncommon for contributory public pension plans to start with contribution rates set somewhat higher and benefits phased in somewhat more slowly than implied by a pure pay-as-you-go pension, with the objective of accumulating enough assets to allow at least partial reserve financing. Most of the plans that began in this way have since evolved toward a pure pay-as-you-go approach, however, either because benefit costs were allowed to rise without the necessary corresponding increases in contribution rates or because the accumulated assets were lost due to war, economic collapse, hyperinflation, mismanagement, or fraud.

Where the public program was relatively modest, another step in the process has been the adoption of policies that *encourage* private supplementation of public pension programs on either a group or individual basis. Such supplementation frequently involves some sort of advance funding and is typically encouraged through favorable tax treatment. These policies are relatively more important where public pension benefits were set substantially below the level required for full replacement of preretirement earnings.

Other countries have evolved by mandating supplementation. In some cases the mandate has taken the form of a new, publicly managed, earnings-related system as a supplement to an earlier universal flat pension. In other cases, the mandate has been directed at the private sector, either directly through legislation or indirectly through publicly sanctioned actions taken by the labor market partners. Mandated private plans are usually (but not always) advance funded. Originally they were more apt to involve group approaches, but countries have more recently begun to mandate individual approaches either exclusively or as an option.

THE CURRENT DEBATE

Public policy debates about the evolution of pensions have focused on different topics, taking on different characteristics at various times over the last hundred years. Philosophical differences about the proper role of government are always a part of any debate. In the past, however, concerns were more likely to center on the effectiveness of different approaches in assuring adequate incomes for the retired.

Current concerns. The current debates seem directed less at ways to improve income adequacy than at ways to alter economic impacts and reflect changes in social philosophies. The precise mix of concerns varies from one part of the world to another, but several common elements appear.

One concern is that under traditional pay-as-you-go pension systems the general level of pension promises has become too generous, the linkages between contributions and benefits are too tenuous, and politically influential groups have been too successful in gaining unjustified privileges. Moreover, whether as a direct result of these trends or of other economic and political developments, the authorities can no longer collect a significant fraction of the pension contributions owed, leaving them unable to finance current pension promises and undermining confidence in their institutions. These concerns are most commonly associated with the systems found in Latin America and the former socialist countries in the early 1990s.

Another concern, common to the developed economies, deals with the cost implications of an aging population, particularly in an environment of slower economic growth. Still other concerns involve the desire to encourage individuals to assume greater responsibility for their own welfare (including responsibility for generating adequate retirement incomes for themselves), the potential that different pension structures may hold for facilitating economic growth, and general disenchantment with the ability of governments to manage important financial institutions. These are frequently encountered in the former socialist countries.

In the current debate, the structural changes discussed most frequently are those that involve moving away from government-managed, pay-as-you-go, defined benefit pension plans to privately managed, advance funded, defined contribution retirement savings plans. The differences between these two approaches stem from perceptions about their ability to address the concerns just noted. Most of the concerns can be addressed without changing all of the characteristics of the pension system. Some concerns involve primarily the difference between advance funding and pay-as-you-go; others involve the difference between defined benefit, group pension plans and individual defined contribution accounts; and some reflect a preference for private management over public management.

Advance funding. The reasons for developing greater reliance on advance funding include the desire to use the pension system as a mechanism for generating additional capital, the hope that such a shift will facilitate the development of efficient, advanced capital markets, and the view that the most likely future environment is one in which advance funding may eventually involve lower contribution rates.[5] Implicitly, advocates of greater reliance on advance funding believe that the kind of economic and international political developments that destroyed past attempts to advance fund pensions are far less likely to occur in the future.

Individual accounts. The emphasis on individual accounts reflects the desire to encourage a greater sense of individual responsibility. Implicit in this is the desire to de-emphasize the pension system's role as a mechanism for promoting social solidarity through redistribution. In those parts of the world where pension benefits were not tied closely to lifetime earnings, a movement to individual accounts can help clarify the linkage between past contributions and future benefits.

Private management. The case for switching to private management rests less on the direct economic consequences of the switch than on questions of general social philosophy and on predictions about the reaction of the political process to different institutional arrangements. Any pension system can rely on individual accounts to closely link contributions and benefits, be it pay-as-you-go or advance funded, publicly or privately managed. Likewise, at least in principle, a system can be advance funded whether it is operated by the private or public sector and whether it is run on a group or an individual basis. The desire for greater reliance on private management of the pension system reflects the concern found in some quarters that a publicly managed system is unlikely to have the discipline to accumulate and maintain a sufficient stock of financial assets and to preserve the close linkage between contributions and benefits. It also reflects, at least in part, a general loss of confidence in the management ability of the public sector, without regard to the advantages or disadvantages of advance funding. The price often paid for shifting to private management, however, is higher administrative costs, particularly in systems that follow the individual saving account model.

MAKING THE TRANSITION TO ADVANCE FUNDING AND INDIVIDUAL ACCOUNTS

Individual accounts. By itself, switching from a group defined benefit plan to a centrally managed retirement plan based on individual accounts is not very difficult. It is mainly a matter of designing a new benefit accrual formula and a strategy for gradually shifting benefit calculations from the old formula to the new. The switch can be accomplished by computing a benefit which represents a weighted average of the two approaches for each worker, with the relative importance of the old approach declining over time. Alternatively, the partial benefits each worker had earned under the old system can simply be converted to reflect the equivalent accrual under the new, individual account approach.

Several recent pension reforms have been based on introducing the individual accounts principle into centrally managed, pay-as-you-go systems, an approach that has become known as a "notional defined contribution" pension plan.[6] In this plan, contributions are accumulated in each individual's account and are credited with interest at a rate approximating the rate at which wages in the economy are growing. At retirement, each individual's benefits are calculated with reference to the balance in his account and paid as a life annuity.

The notional defined contribution approach produces a benefit result similar to that generated by a system that scales retirement benefits directly to years of service and lifetime average (wage adjusted) earnings. The major difference is that the notional approach employs a vocabulary that emphasizes the contribution-benefit linkage.

Advance funding. Introducing advance funding into a contributory pension system is also not a difficult technical matter. The usual approach is to compute the contribution rate needed to finance the benefits of workers newly entering employment covered by the plan and add to it an amount calculated to allow amortizing the unfunded liabilities associated with all workers already in the plan over a fixed period of time, commonly 20 to 30 years. The challenge, of course, is to find the additional resources needed for amortizing the unfunded liability.

Decentralized, individual accounts. The transition to a decentralized system of privately managed individual accounts is much more complex.

It involves developing both a process for transferring the responsibility for managing the accounts and paying the benefits from the public to the private sector and a strategy for amortizing the liabilities associated with the pay-as-you-go scheme.

Typically, those who are already retired when the transition begins are left in the old system, those who enter the labor force after the transition begins are assigned to the new system, and those who are in between are given the option of staying in the old system or moving to the new.[7] The retirement benefits of the workers who transferred mid-career will be comprised in part of the benefit rights earned under the old system and in part of those earned under the new system.

Two approaches have been used to handle mid-career workers who elect (or are required) to switch. Under one approach, such workers are given a recognition bond to reflect the rights accrued under the old system, adjusted for changes in the price level between the date of the transfer and the date of retirement.[8] These bonds become an asset in the worker's new account and are redeemed when the worker reaches retirement age. Under this approach, responsibility for the worker's retirement benefit is transferred completely to the new system at the time the recognition bond is issued.

Under the second approach, responsibility for these workers' retirement benefits is shared. Although no additional benefits are earned in the old system, all or a portion of the rights already acquired are retained in the public system and, at retirement, a benefit that reflects the updated value of these accrued rights is paid. For workers who transfer to the new system, all new accruals occur under the system of individual accounts, and the benefit reflecting their value is paid by the new pension institution.

THE FISCAL CHALLENGE IN SHIFTING TO FUNDED ACCOUNTS

The fiscal challenge of the transition to advance funded individual accounts is finding the resources needed to cover the pension system's current liabilities. As workers are shifted to the new system of individual accounts, their contribution income is no longer available to finance the current benefits of those already retired or the payments that will have to be made in the future on account of benefits already accrued by current workers. A new source of revenue must be found to finance these liabilities.

In a mature social security system, the pension liabilities that would have to be financed in this kind of reform are often well in excess of the entire gross domestic product of the country and of several multiples of the total government budget. Table 1 contains recent IMF estimates of the aggregate amount of these liabilities in some of the major industrial countries.

The first column of numbers in table 1 shows the estimate of the total liability in each country if all of the workers currently under the pay-as-you-go public pension programs in that country were transferred immediately to a new system of individual accounts. Across all eight countries, such a change would leave the pay-as-you-go system with liabilities whose 1995 present value is estimated to average 1.5 times the 1995 gross domestic product of these countries.

Table 1
Estimated Gross Public Pension Liabilities in Major Industrial Countries
(As a percent of 1995 GDP)

	Total	Present Retirees	Current Workers
Eight Major Industrial Countries	151.8	65.1	86.7
United States	101.7	31.7	70.0
Japan	140.3	67.7	72.6
Germany	219.9	106.2	113.7
France	264.5	128.2	136.3
Italy	357.4	170.8	186.6
United Kingdom	116.7	44.8	71.9
Canada	62.8	43.7	19.1
Sweden	105.1	52.9	52.2

Source: Sheetal K. Chand and Albert Jaeger, "Aging Populations and Public Pension Schemes," Occasional Paper 147 (Washington, D.C.: International Monetary Fund, December, 1996).

Note: Liabilities shown are those for a "sudden transition" under which all accruals under the old system stop immediately.

The second and third columns in the table show how the total liability is divided between the amount owed to current retirees and the amount owed to current workers. Slightly less than half of the total estimated liability, averaging some 65 percent of GDP, represents benefit payments to those already retired, while the rest, averaging some 87 percent of GDP, represents liabilities for past benefit accruals of those still working.

Liability estimates vary dramatically according to the age structure and relative generosity of each country's public pension program. Liabilities in the U.K. and the U.S. are just a little over 100 percent of GDP, those of

France and Germany are over 200 percent of GDP, and Italy's is more than 300 percent.[9]

Chart 3 gives an indication of the pace at which these liabilities could come due.[10] The chart assumes that total liabilities are equal to 150 percent of GDP, divided among current retirees and current workers as indicated by the eight-country average in table 1, and that the changeover involves moving all of the current contribution rate from supporting the pay-as-you-go system to supporting the individual accounts.

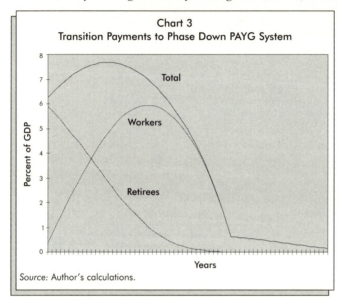

Source: Author's calculations.

The initial challenge is financing the pensions of workers retired at the time the transition occurs. If the present value of these liabilities totals about 65 percent of GDP, payments to current retirees will start at around 6 percent of GDP. They will gradually decline as members of the group die off.

The second stream in chart 3 is the liabilities accrued prior to the transition by those working under the pension program at the time the transition occurred. Those who are approaching retirement age at the time of the transition will have accrued a substantial amount of benefits under the old system. As they begin retiring, the aggregate amount of their liabilities rises. As time passes, however, newly retiring workers will have worked for fewer and fewer years under—and be entitled to progressively smaller payments from—the old program. The last payments under the old program can continue, however, for 75 or more years after the transition, until the death of the last worker who had accrued rights under that program.[11] If the present value of the total liability of this group is roughly 85 percent of GDP at the time of the transition, payments to this group can be expected to rise over the first 25 years, peaking in the neighborhood of 6 percent of GDP, then decline thereafter.

Argentina and Chile are both in the process of paying off liabilities accrued under their pay-as-you-go pension systems, Chile having started in 1981 and Argentina in 1994. The transition deficits associated with these two reforms are shown in chart 4. While substantial, the aggregate public pension liabilities that had to be financed in the transition of each of these countries represented a smaller percentage of GDP than would be the case in most OECD countries. In each case, transition liabilities were reduced when the new system began, via reforms which raised retirement ages and reduced benefit entitlements. Further, the new system in Argentina is a mixed system that preserves a pay-as-you-go base pension to be combined with the new mandatory individual accounts.

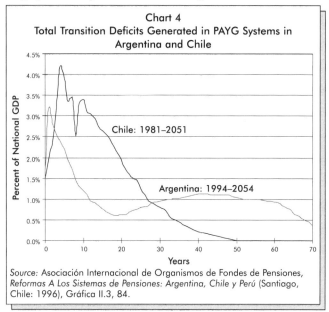

Chart 4
Total Transition Deficits Generated in PAYG Systems in Argentina and Chile

Source: Asociación Internacional de Organismos de Fondes de Pensiones, *Reformas A Los Sistemas de Pensiones: Argentina, Chile y Perú* (Santiago, Chile: 1996), Gráfica II.3, 84.

METHODS OF FINANCING

Financing these deficits will present any country contemplating such a reform with a major fiscal challenge. Basically, the available approaches are the same as those for any other government expenditure: reductions in spending in other accounts, increases in other forms of taxation, and borrowing.

If the primary objective of pension reform is to generate additional capital, transition liabilities must be financed either through tax increases or spending reductions. Either strategy should force a reduction in the aggregate consumption of people living at the time of the transition, which is the only way that aggregate savings in the economy (and hence aggregate capital formation) can increase. The precise incidence of this transition cost will depend on the particular pattern of tax increases and spending cuts enacted. Savings will not increase if the liabilities are financed through increased government borrowing. Instead, the assets accumulating in the workers' accounts will be offset by the rising government debt load, leaving the total stock of capital in the economy largely unaffected.

It is not clear how financial markets would react to the attempt to finance liabilities of this magnitude almost entirely though the issuance of new debt. A likely result would be that markets would demand a higher interest rate on all of the obligations of the national government, including both these new obligations and the previous national debt. In this event, the higher debt service costs on the entire national debt would be an additional cost to the transition.

Even if these liabilities could be debt-financed without causing an increase in the cost of servicing the rest of the national debt, financing the transition is likely to lead to a tax increase eventually. As a part of the analysis that produced the pension liability estimates reported in table 1, IMF staff economists Sheetal K. Chand and Albert Jaeger compared the impact of different strategies for dealing with projected pension financing problems on the finances of the major industrial countries. They found that the cost to government just to service the debt generated by a shift to individual accounts was likely to be greater than the cost of establishing sustainable contribution rates under their pay-as-you-go pension plans.

The results of their analysis are illustrated in table 2. On average, these major industrial countries need to improve their fiscal position (i.e., increase taxes or reduce spending) by 0.3 percent of GDP just to stabilize the ratio of conventional debt to GDP. As of 1995, the largest required adjustments were those of Sweden and Canada; Germany and Italy had already surpassed this particular target. Having stabilized the ratio of conventional debt to GDP, these countries would, on average, have to further improve their fiscal positions (i.e., additional tax/contribution increases or spending reductions) by 1.8 percent of GDP in order to stabilize their pay-as-you-go pension programs. (In this case, stabilizing means establishing a constant contribution rate capable of financing the program for 70 years and beyond.) If, instead, they decided to make a transition to individual defined contribution accounts financed entirely through borrowing, they would have to improve their fiscal position (increase taxes or reduce spending) by an average of 3.8 percent of GDP, 2.0 percent of GDP more than would be required to put the PAYG schemes on a sustainable basis. In effect, the reduction that moving to individual accounts might cause in pension contribution rates is offset by higher general fund taxes that must be paid in order to service the debt created by the transition.

Table 2
Budget Adjustments Required to Ensure Stable Debt/GDP Ratios
(As a percent of 1995 GDP)

Country	Actual Primary Fiscal Balance in 1995*	Change in Primary Balance Needed To Stablilize Current Debt	Additional Change in Primary Balance Required to Stabilize PAYG Pensions	Additional Change in Primary Balance Required to Gradually Phase Out PAYG System
Major Industrial Countries	0.7	0.3	1.8	3.8
United States	0.4	0.7	0.8	2.7
Japan	-0.2	0.5	3.3	4.2
Germany	2.4	-1.3	3.4	6.2
France	-0.3	1.0	3.3	7.1
Italy	3.3	-1.2	2.5	4.3
United Kingdom	0.4	0.3	0.1	1.8
Canada	0.2	2.5	2.0	2.6
Sweden	-5.1	5.2	0.9	3.1

Source: Sheetal K. Chand and Albert Jaeger, "Aging Populations and Public Pension Schemes," Occasional Paper 147 (Washington, D.C.: International Monetary Fund, December, 1996), and author's calculations.

*Primary balance is defined as the fiscal position of the government excluding debt service costs.

Conclusions

Pension programs exist, first and foremost, to provide some assurance of adequate incomes in retirement. Pension arrangements mature at different speeds, however, affecting the pace at which the retirement income objective is achieved. Universal programs are the most effective in quickly improving the income of the aged. Defined benefit approaches can be effective in supplying retirement incomes to those approaching retirement age at the time the plan is adopted, but not those who have already retired. Advance funded defined contribution plans are the slowest to mature, requiring over half a century to approach their full potential as a source of retirement income. Each society's initial retirement income institutions will reflect its views about the importance of the speed at which the system matures, along with its own unique balance of a number of other important social and philosophical issues.

Pension institutions evolve in response to changing economic, demographic, and social conditions. Many systems which were begun using one approach have evolved into mixed or "multi-pillar" approaches. Common elements include assistance programs, government-run pension programs, mandated pension programs operated by private sector institutions, and voluntary group and individual retirement programs.

Currently, there is widespread debate about the merits of de-emphasizing government-run, pay-as-you-go, defined benefit pensions in favor of greater reliance on privately run, individual, defined contribution arrangements. A transition of this sort is very difficult, however, because it requires either paying off the liability for the pension promises in the old system or converting them into explicit public debt while at the same time transferring responsibility for operating the pension system to a new set of institutions.

One objective that advocates of such a transition hope to achieve is enhanced capital formation. This objective cannot be achieved unless the liabilities of the pay-as-you-go system are paid off through some combination of higher taxes and lower government spending on other programs. Even this does not guarantee that capital formation will increase.

The strategy for handling the liabilities under the old system is also important in determining the impact on the aggregate tax burden. A defined contribution system may require lower contribution rates than a pay-as-you-go system in an environment of slowly growing wages and relatively high interest rates. This advantage may easily disappear, however, if the government incurs substantially higher debt service costs in trying to finance the liabilities of the pay-as-you-go system. Regardless of how the liabilities of the pay-as-you-go system are handled, phasing the system out will increase the fiscal pressure on the central government. The process is not a short-range solution to a government's fiscal problems; if anything, it will make them worse.

NOTES

1. As is discussed subsequently, a variant known as "notional defined contribution" has recently been adopted in several countries and proposed in several others. For the purposes of the issues discussed in this chapter, those accounts can be thought of as a variation of the pay-as-you-go defined benefit approach.

2. Except as otherwise noted, the analyses presented here are based on a version of the simple model used in the discussion of the mathematics of pension contribution rates.

The examples assume a population that does not change (births are the same each year, and are the same as deaths), a net interest rate 2 percent higher than the rate of growth of wages, work careers that begin at age 23 and continue through age 64, and a life expectancy at age 65 of 17 years. The examples ignore the possibility of death before retirement.

3. In chart 1, the example used to illustrate a pay-as-you-go system assumes that early cohorts of workers are eligible for benefits if they have worked at least three years under the program. Although it is not unusual to allow the initial cohorts to qualify after only a few years, subsequent cohorts usually need to meet increasing minimum service requirements. Most systems eventually require each cohort to have at least 10 years of service to receive benefits.

4. As was noted in the chapter on the mathematics of pension contribution rates, the aggregate size of the assets accumulated in this kind of system depends on the level of interest, wage growth, and population growth rates, as well as life expectancy at retirement. Variations in these factors will also cause slight variations in how aggregate assets are divided among the worker accounts and retiree accounts. With benefits set to equal one-half of average earnings, a life expectancy at retirement of roughly 17 years and a 43-year work career, when the system matures, aggregate balances in individual accounts are likely to range from four to seven times aggregate wages in the economy, with approximately two-thirds of the total in the accounts of workers and one-third in the accounts of retirees.

5. Each of these three objectives is discussed elsewhere. The first two are covered in the chapter on the impact of pensions on saving and investment and the third is discussed in the chapter on the mathematics of pension contribution rates.

6. See, for example, the discussion of the reforms in Italy and Sweden in chapter 2 of "Developments and Trends in Social Security, 1993–1995," *International Social Security Review* 49:2 (1996), 5–126.

7. In some of the recent Latin American reforms, however, a reformed pay-as-you-go system is also available as an option for new entrants to the labor force. Some of the issues involved in structuring the options to be offered to current mid-career workers are discussed in Robert Holzmann, "On the Economic Benefits and Fiscal Requirements of Moving from Unfunded to Funded Pensions," Research Report 4 (Washington, D.C.: American Institute for Contemporary German Studies, The Johns Hopkins University, 1997).

8. In Chile, such bonds also earn 4 percent real interest, but no interest is paid on recognition bonds in Peru. The value of the bond may or may not be as high as the accrued rights under the old system. Bonds are apt to be less than the accrued benefits where the old system had promised benefits in excess of what society was willing to finance. In Latin America, the conversion to individual accounts has usually been accompanied by an increase in retirement ages and other retrenchments that probably would also have been necessary if the pay-as-you-go scheme had continued.

9. Estimates show smaller liabilities in Canada and Sweden in part because these estimates apply only to the earnings-related portion of each country's public pension program. Both Canada and Sweden also pay a flat, universal pension to virtually all aged residents.

10. Chart 3 traces the pace of benefit payments based on current entitlements assuming a life table for U.S. males born in 1960 and a 3.5 percent real interest rate (the rate used in the IMF calculations). Converting the liabilities into recognition bonds would cause them to come due more quickly.

11. The advantage of using recognition bonds is that the accrued liabilities under the old program are paid off at the time the workers enter retirement so that the transition period ends when the last worker retires, not when he dies. The disadvantage is that the payments must be made earlier.

Chapter Nine

Risks of Mid-Career Economic and Demographic Changes

The contribution rates needed to finance a given pension are determined by the economic and demographic environment, but the particular way in which that environment influences pension contributions depends on the type of pension institution.[1] Under the advance funded approaches, contribution rates are sensitive to the relationship between the rate of growth of wages and the interest rate, but are not affected by changes in birth rates. In contrast, under a pay-as-you-go, defined benefit approach, contribution rates are sensitive to change in the birth rate and are relatively insensitive to changes in interest rates or in the rate of increase in wages.[2] Contribution rates under both approaches are sensitive to changes in life expectancy at retirement.

Each of these economic and demographic variables can be expected to follow an uncertain and changing path over the course of an indiviudal's work career. Every time they change, the contribution rate needed to finance a given retirement pension also changes, leading to changes either in the amount the working-age population must contribute for a given pension or in the amount of pension associated with a given level of contributions. Although the economic and demographic environments cannot be known in advance, the contribution rate must be established to reflect the best information then available about future developments and modified as new information becomes available. For individual participants, however, this means that the contribution rate actually prevailing during working years may turn out to be either too high or too low to produce the target pension at the point that retirement age is reached.

The importance of mid-career changes in the economic and demographic environments depends on how unpredictable actual trends turn out to be and how wide the fluctuations are from one year to the next. To gain an appreciation for the possible magnitude, the impact of the kind of economic and demographic variations that actually occurred in four major economies over the period 1953–95 are simulated here. Over the last four decades, the economies of the major OECD countries have experienced one of the longest periods on record of sustained economic growth uninterrupted by war, depression, hyperinflation, or other major upheaval. The range of the variation in the economic and demographic environment in these relatively stable years was enough, however, to introduce substantial uncertainty into the operation of any of these pension approaches.

THE IMPACT OF MISESTIMATES

Misestimates of the required contribution rates have quite different implications under different pension approaches. Under a defined contribution, individual savings approach, pension benefits are determined solely by the total amount contributed and the investment returns earned on it. Any difference between the contribution rate actually used and the rate that should have been used (regardless of the reason for the discrepancy) creates a gap between the actual asset accumulation and the amount necessary to produce the target pension benefit. The retiree either over- or undershoots the target. Retirees who overshoot the target will have saved too much. They will be able to enjoy higher-than-anticipated retirement incomes, but at the cost of having made greater sacrifices during their working years than were necessary. Retirees who undershoot will be forced to live in retirement with less than they had anticipated.

Under a pay-as-you-go, defined benefit approach, pension benefits are paid as life annuities whose amount is defined in terms of the individual's prior earnings and years of service. In the absence of *ad hoc* adjustments in the formula, the defined benefit attribute insulates pensions from unanticipated changes in earnings, investment returns, or life expectancy at retirement. Because financing is pay-as-you-go, however, it is sensitive to changes in the ratio of beneficiaries to contributors. Changes in birth and mortality rates or in the ratio of the employed population to the total population create mismatches between aggregate contribution income and aggregate benefit expenditure. These are typically resolved through some mixture of changes in contribution rates, changes in the amount of any subsidy from the general budget, changes in the benefit formula applicable to newly retiring workers, and changes in the procedures used for adjusting the benefits of current recipients. In effect, the impact of unanticipated demographic developments is spread among current contributors, current pensioners, future pensioners, and (to the extent that they are a different group) general taxpayers in a pattern that is determined on an *ad hoc* basis by the political process.[3]

THE GENERAL ANALYTICAL APPROACH

The analysis consists of simulating the impact of different economic, demographic, and political developments on pension entitlements. Actual historical data are used to simulate how the wage rate/interest rate relationship, the rate of growth of the population, and mortality rates might change over the course of a worker's career. Several different decision rules are used to set initial contribution rates and to adjust these rates in response to emerging experience. Simulations of economic variations are run using the wage rate/interest rate relationship as it actually unfolded and in exactly the opposite order of the way it actually unfolded. The assumption is that changes of the magnitude observed historically can easily occur again, and that the trend could go in either direction. Simulations of variations in population growth consider only the actual historical experience and current projections.

The historical evidence employed in the analysis is that from the period 1953–95 in Japan, Germany,[4] the United Kingdom, and the United States. In effect, the analysis illustrates the retirement pensions that might have been generated for an individual whose work career spanned these 43 years.

The economic and demographic experience in these countries is summarized in tables 1 and 2.[5] Over the first two decades of the period, wages grew relatively rapidly everywhere except the U.S., and real interest rates were fairly low. (Even in the U.S., the real wage growth rate exceeded the real interest rate over the period 1953–73.) In the later two decades, wage growth slowed and real interest rates rose in all four countries. Since

Table 1
Real Wage Growth, Interest Rates, and Implied Individual Account Contribution Rates in Four OECD Countries

Periods	Germany			Japan			U.K.			U.S.		
	Wage Growth	Int. Rate	CR	Wage Growth	Int. Rate	CR	Wage Growth	Int. Rate	CR	Wage Growth	Int. Rate	CR
1st 10 yrs (1953–62)	8.4	3.8	64.2	9.5	5.3	57.7	5.8	1.0	70.5	2.7	1.4	28.6
2nd 10 yrs (1963–72)	6.1	3.9	36.0	7.7	4.3	47.8	5.2	2.5	41.7	1.8	-0.6	39.0
3rd 10 yrs (1973–82)	3.4	3.0	22.4	2.2	2.8	16.6	1.3	-1.2	40.7	-1.2	2.9	5.2
4th 10 yrs (1983–92)	2.7	5.0	9.8	1.3	3.5	9.9	2.7	4.1	13.1	1.0	5.0	5.7
First 21 yrs (1953–73)	7.1	3.8	48.5	8.5	4.6	54.2	5.4	1.7	53.5	2.2	0.3	33.4
Next 22 yrs (1974–95)	2.6	4.0	12.9	1.8	3.0	14.0	1.8	1.9	19.0	-0.1	4.1	5.1
Full 43 yrs (1953–95)	4.8	3.9	25.5	5.0	3.8	28.1	3.6	1.8	32.2	1.0	2.3	13.5

Source: International Monetary Fund, *International Yearbook of Financial Statistics*, 1996; U.S. Bureau of Labor Statistics, Department of Commerce, http://stat.bls.gov; and author's calculations. Interest rates are for 10-year government bonds.

Table 2
Population Growth Rates in Four OECD Countries
(percentages)

	Germany	Japan	U.K.	U.S.
Total Population				
1950–59	0.66	1.11	0.39	1.73
1960–69	1.29	1.14	0.60	1.27
1970–79	1.50	1.13	0.07	1.06
1980–89	-0.10	0.48	0.08	0.88
1990–99	-0.22	0.37	0.12	0.66
2030–39	-0.72	-0.18	-0.16	0.19
Working-Age Population				
1950–55	1.34	1.95	-0.10	0.71
1990–95	-0.50	0.21	-0.04	0.71
2020–25	-1.12	-0.19	-0.49	-0.27

Source: Robert P. Hagemann and Giuseppe Nicoletti, "Population Ageing: Economic Effects and Some Policy Implications for Financing Public Pensions," OECD Economic Studies 12 (Spring 1989), table 1, 54; and United Nations, *World Population Prospects, 1988*, Population Studies 106 (New York: Department of International Economic and Social Affairs).

1973, the real interest rate has consistently been higher than the rate of growth of real wages in three of the four countries; in Japan, it was higher than the real wage growth rate until 1993.

In all four countries, the rate of growth of population tended first to accelerate and then to slow, although the timing was slightly different in each country. In the U.S. and the U.K., the slowing of population growth is evident in the 1970s. In Germany and Japan, it is more obvious in the 1980s. Projections into the future suggest further slowing of population growth rates in all four countries in the first third of the next century.

For pension finance purposes, the rate of growth of the population of working age is probably more important than the rate of growth of the total population. Growth rates of the working-age population at three different points in time in each of these countries are also shown in table 2. By the 1990s, the working-age population was growing much more slowly in both Germany and Japan than it had been in the early 1950s, but this pattern did not occur in either the U.K. and the U.S. Projections show that growth rates will slow in all four countries over the next 30 years, however.

To keep the analysis simple, it is based on the same basic model used in the discussion of the mathematics of pension contribution rates. In this model, people enter the labor force at age 22 and are employed consistently at the average wage for the following 43 years. All workers retire at age 65 and they all die on their 82nd birthday. The target pension for each worker is equal to one-half of the average wage, indexed after retirement to reflect changes in prevailing wage levels. The objective of the exercise is to apply plausible decision rules about how contribution rates would be set and see how close people come to achieving this target pension. For the purpose of these calculations, administrative costs are ignored.

VARIATIONS IN THE ECONOMIC ENVIRONMENT

It is immediately clear from table 1 that the contribution rates required to produce the target pension are extraordinarily sensitive to the economic environment. Actual experience at several points in the history of these countries saw wage growth so high relative to real interest rates that the contribution rate required under the simple model runs some 50 percent or more (e.g., the 1950s in Japan, Germany, and the U.K. and the 1960s in Japan). At other times, wage growth was so slow relative to the level of interest rates that the target pension could have been produced with a contribution rate of less than 10 percent (e.g., the 1970s and 1980s in the U.S. and the 1980s in Germany and Japan).

Variability when long-term trends are known. The first set of simulations was based on the assumption that the authorities know how real wages and interest rates will behave in the long run, but do not know what kind of year-to-year fluctuations to expect. The results of these simulations employing the actual economic data applicable to these four countries are shown in the first panel of table 3. (Country identifications in

Table 3
Impact of Different Strategies for Setting Contribution Rates for Individual Accounts
(Simulated Actual Asset Balance at Retirement as a Percent of the Balance Required to Produce the Target Pension)
(100% bonds; all values in percent, except where indicated)

	Germany	Japan	U.K.	U.S.
Simulation 1. Contribution rate set at level appropriate for long-term (43-year) trend				
Actual Sequence	137	132	140	138
Reverse Sequence	88	80	73	80
Simulation 2. Contribution rate set at level appropriate for first half				
Actual Sequence	261	255	233	342
Reverse Sequence	41	40	43	30
Simulation 3. Contribution rate adjusted every 10 years (in line with economic conditions of preceding 10 years)				
Actual Sequence	163	153	165	181
Reverse Sequence	66	68	64	58
Basic Data				
43-year average wage increase	4.8	5.0	3.6	1.0
43-year average interest rate	3.9	3.8	1.8	2.3
Ratio of target accumulation to average wage (no units)	9.2	9.5	9.9	7.6

Source: Calculations based on data in appendix table A.

these simulations are intended as a means of identifying the particular wage and interest pattern being simulated, not a prediction of the results that might actually apply in any particular country.)

The simulations start with the calculation of the stock of assets that will be needed at age 65 in order to meet the pension target of 50 percent of average wages (shown at the bottom of table 2). The required asset stock is itself dependent on long-term economic trends, and is calculated based on the 43-year average of real wage growth and interest rates for each country. For example, in this basic model, financing a wage-indexed pension equal to 50 percent of average wages for 17 years would require, at age 65, a stock of assets equal to 9.2 times average earnings in the economic environment that prevailed in Germany, 9.5 times average earnings in the Japanese environment, and so forth.

The next step is calculating the stock of assets that would be accumulated if someone actually worked each of the 43 years at the average wage, made contributions at the rate implied by the long-term economic trends, and earned interest each year on the accumulated contributions at the prevailing interest rate. This calculation is performed twice for each country, once assuming the year-to-year fluctuations in wage growth and interest rates that actually occurred and once assuming the exact reverse order of the actual year-to-year sequence.

As the results indicate, the timing of the variations has a significant effect on the size of the asset stock accumulated. In these simulations, the contribution rate that is appropriate based on the 43-year average produces a stock of assets that is 30 to 40 percent too high using the actual sequence of events, and produces a stock of assets that is 15 to 25 percent too low using the reverse of the actual sequence. These simulations suggest that, even if the long-term average were predicted perfectly, year-to-year variations in the values that produce the annual average would cause actual pensions to differ substantially from the target. Instead of replacing 50 percent of preretirement earnings, pensions could run anywhere from 37.5 percent to 75 percent of preretirement earnings.

Variability when long-term trends are not known. The second set of simulations shown in the middle panel of table 3 introduces slightly more realism by relaxing the assumption that the authorities could make a perfect forecast of long-term economic developments over a 43-year period. In this second set, the authorities can only predict with certainty how the economy will perform for the first two decades, and they set contribution rates accordingly. Although they predict the long-term trend correctly for the first two decades, they do not foresee subsequent developments.

As is shown in the middle panel, this decision rule produces large gaps between the actual asset accumulation and the target. When annual fluctuations are introduced in the actual sequence, the contribution rate established proves to be much too high and results in asset accumulations that are two to three times as much as needed for the target pension. In contrast, when annual fluctuations are introduced in the reverse of the actual sequence, the contribution rate established based on perfect foresight of the first two decades proves to be much too low and results in asset accumulations that are only 30 to 40 percent of the target. In this simulation, variations in the actual course of economic events cause pensions to range from 15 to 170 percent of preretirement earnings.

The third panel presents results based on a simulation which was designed to introduce even more realism into the analysis. These results come from simulating a procedure in which the contribution rate is adjusted each decade to reflect the actual experience of the previous decade. In this simulation, the contribution rate for the first 10 years is set at the level used in the first set of simulations—the rate appropriate when long-term average rates of increase in wages and interest rates are known with certainty. Every 10 years thereafter, however, the contribution rate is adjusted either upward or downward to reflect the contribution rate that would have been appropriate based on the economic environment of the previous decade. The adjustments are assumed to occur at the pace of a 0.5 percentage point change in the contribution rate each year until the new rate is reached (or the decade ends).

The results shown in the third panel of table 3 indicate that while this rule produces better results than did the previous rule, the excess contribution is still substantial. When simulated using the actual annual fluctuations, this procedure causes asset accumulations of as much as 80 percent in excess of the target. When the simulation uses the reverse of the actual fluctuations, the asset accumulations fall short of the target by some 30 to 40 percent.

Combining stocks and bonds. The results discussed thus far are based on simulations in which assets are assumed to be invested at the rate of interest prevailing each year on 10-year government bonds. Appendix table B shows how these results change when each of the simulations is repeated assuming instead that asset holdings are divided equally between 10-year government bonds and equities.[6] Introducing equity returns increases the average return that workers can expect, thereby allowing a lower contribution rate. It also introduces somewhat more volatility into the year-to-year pattern of asset returns.

The greater volatility associated with the investment in equities does not introduce greater variation in the results of these simulations, however. Introducing equities causes accumulations to become somewhat less predictable in the context of the economic history of the U.K. and somewhat more predictable in the context of the U.S. economic data. In the context of the economic data from Germany, and to a lesser extent Japan, the introduction of equity returns narrows the range of variation.

Equity investment magnifies another problem that is not as serious when portfolios are held mostly in bonds. With equity investment, the value of the pension available to a given retiree is quite sensitive to the exact year in which the individual reaches retirement age, owing to the greater volatility in the value of the asset portfolio. Those who reach retirement age when asset markets are depressed will find that their assets buy a much more modest pension than those who are fortunate enough to reach retirement age when asset markets are unusually high.

Simulations using these same historical data suggest that when retirement portfolios are held entirely in bonds, the retirement pension associated with the portfolios accumulated by the average member of any one retirement cohort can be expected to vary by only about 3 percent from the value of the portfolios accumulated by the average member of an adjacent cohort (see table 4).[7] When half of the portfolio is held in equities, however, the average variation among adjacent cohorts increases substantially, to just over 9 percent. In the case where half the portfolio is in equities, if the average worker in one cohort received a pension equal to the target of 50 percent of average earnings, an identical worker in the next cohort could expect, on average, to get a pension that represented either 46 percent or 54 percent of average earnings. In some years, there would be less variance; in other years there would be more.[8]

Table 4
Simulated Impact of a One-Year Variation in Year of Retirement
(Mean absolute percentage difference in the ratio of retirement benefits to preretirement earnings among adjacent retirement cohorts)

	Germany	Japan	U.K.	U.S.	All Four
Bonds Only					
Mean Difference	3.2	3.6	3.4	2.8	3.2
Standard Deviation	1.9	3.4	1.7	1.6	2.2
50% Bonds and 50% Stocks					
Mean Difference	11.6	9.6	7.6	8.1	9.2
Standard Deviation	10.7	6.5	4.6	5.5	7.2

Source: Calculations based on data in appendix table A.

VARIATIONS IN THE DEMOGRAPHIC ENVIRONMENT

Changes in mortality. Regardless of the pension approach employed, an increase in the amount of time that newly retiring workers can expect to live in retirement will raise the cost of providing them with a given monthly income. When this occurs, the choices facing *new entrants* to the labor force are the same under all pension approaches. Either they must make higher contributions during their working years, extend their work lives, or accept a lower retirement income. The approaches differ, however, in their treatment of those who are currently in *mid-career* when life expectancies increase.

Life expectancies at age 65 have increased substantially in many parts of the world since the Second World War, causing populations to age and pension costs to rise. Japan provides a particularly dramatic example. Between 1953 and 1990, life expectancy at age 65 for Japanese men increased by 40 percent, from 11.8 years to 16.7 years. In a system based on defined contribution, individual accounts, contribution rates that would have produced an adequate retirement benefit for a Japanese worker with 1953 life expectancy would produce only 70 to 75 percent of what was needed to finance the target retirement income at 1990 life expectancies.[9] In the United States, a man who contributed on the basis of 1953 life expectancies would experience a shortfall of just over 10 percent due to changes in retiree life expectancy occurring over his lifetime.

The two pension approaches differ in the likely impact on pension benefits of these mortality improvements occurring in the middle of an individual's work career. In the defined contribution, individual account approach, such mortality improvements will most likely be translated entirely into reductions in monthly retirement benefits.[10] In a pay-as-you-go system, these kinds of mortality improvements will cause financing difficulties and force either increases in contribution rates or reductions in benefit entitlements. The precise pattern of adjustments will be determined in the political process, and is likely to feature some combination of the two approaches. Moreover, benefit reductions are themselves likely to be divided among the currently retired population, those about to retire, and those just entering the workforce. In this way, the impact of changes in post-retirement mortality are spread among the population as a whole.

Changes in birth rates. Changes in post-retirement mortality have essentially the same effect on the relationship between contribution and pension levels under all pension approaches, but changes in birth rates do not. A slowdown in population growth traceable to a decline in birth rates will force contribution rates to rise (or benefits to fall) under a pay-as-you-go approach, but will have no direct impact on the financing of defined contribution pensions. When such a change occurs during an individual's working life, the result can be that benefit expectations under the pay-as-you-go plan are upset, whereas those under the defined contribution approach are not.

The potential magnitude of this kind of demographic change was indicated earlier by the data in table 2. For example, the working-age population in Germany was growing at an average annual rate of 1.34 percent per year in the early 1950s, but declining at an average annual rate of 0.5 percent per year during the early 1990s. It is projected to decline even more rapidly in the third decade of the next century. Similarly, the working-age population grew quite rapidly in Japan in the early 1950s, but growth had slowed by the early 1990s and further declines are projected.

Changes of the magnitude implied by Germany's population growth numbers would cause the pay-as-you-go rate needed to finance the target pension in the simple model used here to rise from 13.1 percent to 22.9 percent over the career of a worker who entered the labor force in 1950. If population projections prove accurate, a worker entering the labor force in 1990 could find that the contribution rate had risen to 27.5 percent by 2025.

The risk to those in mid-career when these kinds of demographic changes occur is that the political system will decide to cut benefits rather than institute further increases in contribution rates. In principle, under a defined benefit pension plan, those contributing to the plan have been promised a certain benefit. In practice, however, when a pay-as-you-go plan has financial problems, one common result is a reduction in the level of benefits promised future retirees.

Calculations in table 5 suggest the possible impacts on retirement benefits under two different assumptions about how demographic changes will

Table 5
Impact of Different Strategies for Adjusting Pensions When Population Growth Slows
(Pensions at retirement as percent of pension expected when work career begins)

	Germany	Japan	U.K.	U.S.
Simulation 1. All of adjustment achieved through reduced benefits				
1995 Retiree	57	58	102	100
2025 Retiree	84	89	87	74
Simulation 2. One-half of adjustment achieved through reduced benefits				
1995 Retiree	79	79	101	100
2025 Retiree	94	96	94	87
Contribution Rates				
PAYG rate (in percent) with no change in benefits				
1950–55	13.1	10.8	20.4	16.0
1990–95	22.9	18.6	20.0	15.9
2020–25	27.5	20.9	22.9	21.4
PAYG rate (in percent) when one-half of adjustment is through reduced benefits				
1950–55	13.1	10.8	20.4	16.0
1990–95	18.0	14.7	20.2	15.9
2020–25	20.3	15.9	21.6	18.7

Source: Calculations based on data in table 2.

affect the benefits of those who are mid-career when the change occurs. The first simulation shown illustrates the maximum possible impact on pension amounts, the impact if all such demographic changes were to be accommodated entirely through benefit reductions. Essentially, workers entering the labor force in the 1950s would find (under the simulation using German demography) that their pensions were only 57 percent of the amount promised them at the beginning of their careers. Under current projections, workers entering the labor force in 1990 appear to face less risk, since the change occurring during their working lives is less dramatic. Whatever the pension promise might have been when they started their careers, under this simulation they will actually receive 84 percent of what was promised.

The assumption that the entire adjustment to slower growth will be in benefits levels seems contrary to the recent experience of most defined benefit pension plans. An alternative adjustment strategy might be to cover half of the cost increase through higher contribution rates and use benefit reductions to close the remaining gap. The second simulation shows how this adjustment process would affect the benefits of those in the middle of their working careers at the time the change occurs. In this case, the simulation using the demographic history of Germany produces a 1990s' benefit equal to 79 percent of the amount that had been promised in 1950. It implies a contribution rate increase of more than one-third.[11]

The demographic changes occurring during individual working careers seem to have been most dramatic in Germany and Japan during the years since 1950; projections in both countries suggest a slowing of the pace of this kind of demographic change over the next three decades.[12] Changes since 1950 in the U.S. and the U.K. have been of little consequence, although significant change is projected for the U.S. between the 1990s and the 2020s. Thus, the kind of potential mid-career benefit changes associated with most of the rest of the situations portrayed in table 5 are less dramatic than the changes in the first of the German examples.

Summary

Pension promises are inherently risky in that changes in the economic and demographic environment over the course of an individual's career can cause the actual benefit at retirement to depart from the levels promised, implicitly or explicitly, at the time the individual entered the labor force.

The pension approaches differ, however, with respect to their particular economic or demographic sensitivities and in the initial impact that demographic and economic changes have on pension benefits.

In pension plans following the defined contribution, individual accounts model, actual pensions are quite sensitive to economic conditions over an individual's work career, as well as to changes in life expectancy at retirement. All of the uncertainty associated with these sources of variation is borne by the individual participant. These pension plans are not particularly sensitive to changes in the rate of growth of population.

In contrast, pension plans following the pay-as-you-go, defined benefit approach are quite sensitive to changes in population growth rates and to changes in life expectancy at retirement, but are not particularly sensitive to changes in economic conditions. In addition, in these plans unexpected demographic developments lead initially to financing problems which must be resolved through political processes. In this way, the risks typically are shared among current retirees, current contributors, and those about to retire.

Increases in retiree life expectancy occurring during an individual's work life can have the effect of reducing expected retirement benefits by 10 percent or more, assuming they are adjusted for completely through benefit changes. The history of the last half-century suggests that uncertainties about future economic developments can easily cause asset accumulations in defined contribution plans to fall one-third short of the initial target and, just as easily, come in twice as high as the target. In either case, the amount by which the initial target was missed will be translated directly into retirement benefits that were higher or lower than expected. The same history suggests that changes in population growth rates can also lead to a shortfall of some 25 to 30 percent in a pay-as-you-go, defined benefit plan. The extent to which this is translated into lower benefits depends on the adjustment strategy adopted through the political process, however.

All pension plans involve risk. On balance, it appears that the risk is greater under the defined contribution approach. The uncertainty associated with future economic developments appears to exert a stronger influence on defined contribution pension finances than the uncertainty of future demographic developments exerts on defined benefit pension finances. Moreover, the uncertainty is borne entirely by the individual participant under the defined contribution approach, whereas adjustments in defined benefit plans usually produce some sharing of risks among those who are already retired, those who are approaching retirement age, and those who will continue to be contributors for a number of years.

Notes

1. See the earlier brief on the mathematics of pension contribution rates.

2. Contribution rates under a pay-as-you-go, defined benefit plan will be sensitive to changes in the rate of growth of real wages if post-retirement benefits are indexed to prices, but this sensitivity is absent when post-retirement benefits are indexed to wages.

3. Although this analysis focuses on the two models discussed here, at least two other models should also be mentioned: advance funded, defined benefit pension plans and the newer pay-as-you-go, notional defined contribution plans. Adjustments in the former are more apt to be reflected in either the costs that must be borne by the pension plan's sponsor (usually one or more private employers) or by changes to the prospective benefits of those still employed. The latter are too new to have dealt with this kind of problem. In principle, however, they automatically keep benefits adjusted to prevailing wage levels in much the same way as a pay-as-you-go, defined benefit plan, but leave the risk of changes in life expectancy at retirement to be assumed by the beneficiary, in much the same way as an advance funded, defined contribution plan.

4. The data apply to the western portion of Germany prior to reunification.

5. Wage data tend to reflect increases in manufacturing wages, and interest rates are for 10-year government bonds. Both are adjusted for changes in consumer prices. The complete economic data are presented in appendix table A.

6. Equity returns include both changes in market prices and dividend yields.

7. These calculations understate the uncertainty associated with investment exclusively in bonds because they ignore capital gains and losses associated with interest rate changes.

8. These results are based on calculations in which the period over which assets could be accumulated was shortened to 33 years (and the contribution rate each year increased accordingly) to allow a comparison among the experiences of 10 consecutive cohorts. All calculations employed the contribution rate appropriate for the respective long-term average economic environment of the country, the same rule used to generate the results shown in the top panel of table 2. Results for the actual sequence and the reverse sequence are combined to produce a total of 20 observations for each country and each investment policy.

9. The estimate of 70 to 75 percent represents the difference between the value of an annuity that could be purchased with a specified sum using the 1950 Japanese male life table and the annuity that could be purchased with the same sum using the 1990 male life

table, assuming a real interest rate of 0 percent and 3.5 percent respectively and ignoring administrative charges.

10. Similarly, in the newer notional defined contribution approaches, the benefit computation process explicitly adjusts monthly benefits for both past and expected future retiree mortality improvements.

11. The new notional defined contribution approaches differ in the method used to adjust future entitlements during a person's work career. The different approaches have significantly different implications when population growth rates change. If the notional account balance is adjusted by the rate of growth of total earnings, a slowing in the rate of growth of the working-age population should translate fairly directly into a slowing in the rate of growth of benefits. If the notional accounts are adjusted at the rate that average earnings are growing, however, the result mirrors that produced by the traditional defined benefit approach. In this case, the impact of demographic changes occurring during a working career will depend on the adjustment strategy adopted through the political process.

12. Projections are inherently risky. Of all of the possible demographic variables that can be projected, however, those of the working-age population some 30 years from now are among the least risky. Most have already been born and, at least in developed countries, mortality rates at younger ages are low and fairly stable.

Appendix Table A
Historical, Inflation-Adjusted Data on Four OECD Countries
(All entries in percent)

	Germany				Japan				U.K.				U.S.			
Year	Inflation Rates	Wage Growth Rates	Interest Rates	Capital Returns	Inflation Rates	Wage Growth Rates	Interest Rates	Capital Returns	Inflation Rates	Wage Growth Rates	Interest Rates	Capital Returns	Inflation Rates	Wage Growth Rates	Interest Rates	Capital Returns
1953	-2.7	9.6	2.9	21.8	10.7	13.0	-0.8	-5.3	1.6	5.0	-1.9	21.2	-1.4	7.2	1.5	1.7
1954	2.8	1.8	3.1	67.7	1.2	7.7	-0.2	-2.8	3.9	4.8	-2.2	36.5	0.3	0.9	1.0	49.8
1955	1.3	12.3	2.3	21.4	-0.9	18.2	3.6	39.0	5.3	4.5	-1.2	1.9	0.0	5.0	1.2	25.3
1956	1.6	7.8	4.5	-5.5	2.7	3.9	4.2	36.7	3.1	8.7	-0.7	-5.9	3.4	5.4	1.4	4.8
1957	2.1	8.7	5.4	7.7	1.8	6.6	6.4	30.6	4.4	9.8	1.3	-1.4	3.0	-0.5	1.9	-13.1
1958	1.1	7.1	5.8	70.4	0.3	1.0	8.1	-0.3	1.7	8.3	2.1	39.3	1.3	-1.9	1.5	43.0
1959	2.2	7.5	4.2	84.7	1.9	9.4	7.4	35.7	0.0	5.7	4.1	50.3	0.3	4.2	2.2	12.7
1960	0.9	9.9	3.9	34.9	3.7	8.0	7.5	41.6	2.2	3.3	4.7	-2.3	0.0	2.2	1.6	0.9
1961	2.7	9.3	3.0	-8.9	9.3	14.7	8.5	-11.8	4.2	3.6	2.7	-1.6	-0.3	1.0	1.0	27.8
1962	2.9	9.9	2.9	-23.4	4.6	13.6	8.9	-0.5	2.5	4.8	1.3	1.3	0.3	4.0	0.8	-10.2
1963	3.4	4.3	3.5	11.1	6.3	16.1	6.2	-8.0	2.0	8.6	3.6	13.3	-0.3	1.1	0.6	21.8
1964	2.1	4.6	2.7	4.3	4.7	8.4	6.0	0.2	4.9	4.2	2.8	-9.7	0.0	2.8	0.1	16.4
1965	4.0	6.5	3.6	-14.2	6.6	15.3	4.8	16.2	4.6	8.5	1.5	7.3	2.2	0.2	-0.8	11.6
1966	2.9	4.6	4.4	-17.1	4.4	11.1	3.9	6.2	3.5	7.8	2.7	-8.8	3.1	3.1	-0.7	-11.6
1967	0.5	4.2	5.3	49.0	5.7	13.1	5.2	-9.8	2.6	6.1	4.4	35.3	0.3	2.4	-0.7	26.4
1968	2.3	2.8	4.8	13.2	3.8	6.0	5.3	31.8	5.8	3.1	2.4	35.1	2.4	2.6	-0.5	10.1
1969	2.1	8.0	4.8	9.2	6.4	7.9	5.1	34.1	4.7	1.7	3.0	-13.3	4.1	0.3	0.1	-13.4
1970	4.0	13.9	4.8	-26.2	8.1	-15.3	3.7	-20.2	7.9	5.0	2.7	-10.4	3.7	-0.7	0.1	-2.3
1971	5.5	7.5	2.7	3.7	4.8	7.6	2.0	33.3	8.7	2.1	-0.1	35.4	3.3	0.6	-1.7	14.0
1972	6.4	4.7	2.3	8.3	5.9	10.2	1.1	95.1	7.7	5.5	1.9	8.0	4.5	6.1	-2.2	12.9
1973	7.8	5.7	2.2	-21.2	18.2	6.5	0.2	-34.1	10.7	3.5	1.3	-35.5	13.1	0.1	-1.6	-27.9
1974	5.7	7.0	3.2	-4.1	21.0	1.4	2.1	6.1	18.9	2.1	-0.7	-59.2	18.9	-4.5	-0.4	-39.8
1975	5.4	5.2	2.4	22.2	8.0	5.5	3.1	-19.8	25.0	1.9	-7.6	100.6	9.2	-1.5	0.8	26.9
1976	3.7	1.5	3.4	-7.2	10.5	2.8	4.2	9.8	15.1	-1.4	-2.1	-11.2	4.6	1.1	0.7	21.0
1977	3.5	4.7	2.4	6.5	5.0	1.2	3.5	-7.9	12.2	-4.9	-3.0	32.7	6.2	-0.4	0.9	-8.3
1978	2.5	3.9	3.0	5.3	3.8	2.9	3.3	21.2	8.4	6.2	3.3	0.1	7.7	0.2	2.0	1.5
1979	5.5	2.8	3.2	-11.4	5.7	1.8	3.4	-1.3	17.2	1.4	-1.8	-5.7	12.6	-2.4	3.5	11.5
1980	5.7	2.9	2.9	-2.0	7.2	-2.0	3.6	2.0	15.2	0.9	-5.1	17.4	14.1	-3.9	6.2	17.1
1981	6.8	1.0	3.8	-3.8	4.3	0.3	2.2	12.1	12.0	1.3	0.9	1.5	9.1	-0.2	9.1	-11.8
1982	4.6	-0.1	3.5	9.2	2.1	2.2	2.6	4.0	5.4	2.5	3.1	22.5	2.0	-0.5	8.8	16.3
1983	2.6	0.8	4.4	24.0	1.7	1.3	4.0	26.1	5.3	3.9	5.4	22.5	1.3	1.8	7.1	21.9
1984	2.0	0.8	5.2	6.4	2.7	1.1	4.3	22.0	4.6	0.7	4.9	26.1	2.4	2.3	8.4	0.7
1985	1.7	1.8	4.6	54.2	1.4	1.2	4.1	14.5	5.6	5.0	3.9	14.0	-0.5	0.7	6.8	33.2
1986	-1.0	5.4	6.0	6.7	-0.3	2.2	5.0	49.7	3.8	4.5	5.9	22.7	-2.9	1.4	4.1	19.6
1987	1.0	4.7	5.6	-30.1	0.9	1.9	4.0	10.3	3.7	3.8	4.9	4.0	2.6	2.7	4.6	-0.3
1988	1.8	2.5	4.7	29.8	1.0	2.8	2.9	35.8	6.8	3.2	4.0	4.1	4.0	0.9	5.5	13.4
1989	3.1	1.4	4.2	32.8	2.6	0.9	2.2	21.0	7.7	1.2	1.3	25.8	5.0	-0.8	4.1	23.1
1990	2.7	2.6	6.0	-16.9	3.8	0.6	4.5	-40.9	9.3	0.3	1.3	-17.5	3.7	-0.6	3.6	-9.5
1991	5.3	3.6	5.0	-0.6	2.7	0.1	2.9	-4.1	4.5	2.0	3.9	15.6	0.2	-0.4	2.9	34.0
1992	3.3	3.0	3.8	-9.4	1.2	0.4	1.1	-24.8	2.6	2.3	5.3	15.7	0.6	2.2	2.7	8.3
1993	4.2	1.8	2.1	38.7	1.0	0.7	-0.1	10.3	1.9	2.6	6.0	26.0	1.5	-1.9	2.3	9.7
1994	2.5	-1.4	3.6	-8.2	0.7	1.6	1.1	8.2	2.9	0.3	5.5	-8.5	1.3	0.2	4.1	-1.3
1995	1.8	0.9	4.8	2.9	-0.3	9.4	1.5	1.4	3.2	-0.2	4.7	20.0	3.6	1.1	3.7	31.7

Source: Price data are from "Consumer Price Indexes, Sixteen Countries, 1950–1995" (U.S. Bureau of Labor Statistics, April 1996). Real wage growth rates were calculated from nominal rates taken from the *International Financial Statistical Yearbook, 1996*, (IFSY) (International Monetary Fund, 1966–95), and manufacturing wage growth indices from the U.S. Bureau of Labor Statistics, Department of Commerce (1953–65). Real interest rates were calculated using 10-year nominal government bond rates from IFSY (1966–96) and data (sources to follow) provided by Global Financial Data, Inc., Alhambra, California: for Germany: *Wirtschaft und Statistik* Bundesbank (1948–55), Organization for Economic Cooperation and Development (OECD) (1956–95); for Japan: Industrial and Commercial Semi-Annual Report (1948–57), Nippon Telephone and Telegraph Bonds (1957–68), OECD (1969–95); for U.K.: Central Statistical Office, *Annual Abstract of Statistics*, London: CSO (1853–95) and the *Financial Times*; for U.S.: Federal Reserve Bank, *National Monetary Statistics*, New York. Real capital returns data (sources to follow) provided by Global Financial Data, Inc., Alhambra, California: for Germany: Statistisches Reichsamt, *Wirtschaft und Statistik*, Berlin (1926–69), Bundesbank and Die Bundesbank, *Statistische Beihefte zu den Monatsberichten der Deutschen Bundesbank*, Reihe 2, Wertpapierstatistik, Frankfurt am Main: Die Bundesbank (1970–95); for Japan: *Japan Statistical Yearbook*, Sorifu: Tokeikyoku (1950–63), Tokyo Stock Exchange, Tokyo Tokei Geppo, Tokyo: Tokyo Shoken Torihikijo Chosaku (1964–95); for U.K.: Central Statistical Office, *Annual Abstract of Statistics*, London: CSO (1939–1988), Eurostat (1989–95) for the *Financial Times* actuaries yields and *The Economist* (1939–65), Central Statistical Office, *Monthly Digest of Statistics*, London: CSO (1966–) for the FTI-30 yields; London and Cambridge Economic Service, *Key Statistics of the British Economy*, London: L&CES, 1966 for earnings yields from 1927 through 1962; for U.S.: *Standard and Poor's Security Price Index*, New York, (1926–95).

APPENDIX TABLE B
Impact of Different Strategies for Setting Contribution Rates for Individual Accounts

(Simulated actual asset balance at retirement as a percent of the balance required to produce the target pension)

(50/50 mix of stocks and bonds; all values in percent, except where indicated)

	Germany	Japan	U.K.	U.S.
Simulation 1. Contribution rate set at level appropriate for long-term (43-year) trend				
Actual Sequence	97	119	132	118
Reverse Sequence	113	97	77	85
Simulation 2. Contribution rate set at level appropriate for first half				
Actual Sequence	125	173	278	253
Reverse Sequence	88	67	35	39
Simulation 3. Contribution rate adjusted every 10 years (in line with economic conditions of preceding 10 years)				
Actual Sequence	93	125	188	154
Reverse Sequence	100	87	59	66
Basic Data				
43-year average wage increase	4.8	5.0	3.6	1.0
43-year average return	6.3	6.7	5.6	5.7
Ratio of target accumulation to average wage (no units)	7.5	7.4	7.1	5.8

Source: Calculations based on data in appendix table A.

Chapter Ten

Ensuring Income Adequacy Throughout Retirement

The income support supplied by most public pension plans comes in the form of monthly benefits which continue for the lifetime of the retiree, no matter how long that may be, and are adjusted from time to time to reflect changes in prevailing wage or price levels that occur after the individual retires. These arrangements offer a degree of assurance to retirees that if they begin their retirement years with an adequate pension, that pension is likely to remain adequate throughout their retirement years.

The guarantees that benefits will be kept current with prevailing wage and price levels are never absolute, however. In most developed countries, these adjustments occur automatically and follow the movements in a previously announced wage or price index, but in many developing countries the adjustments are made on an *ad hoc* basis, commonly in connection with legislated changes in minimum wages. Even where indexing is automatic, the adjustments are occasionally modified during periods of economic distress to reflect fiscal realities.

Privately managed, defined benefit pension plans almost always offer monthly benefits throughout the remaining life of the retiree, at least as an option. Policies for adjusting these monthly benefits after retirement are more varied, however. Such adjustments are regular and predictable in some countries but relatively rare in others. They tend to be more common where the privately managed plans provide a major portion of the retirement incomes for a majority of the population and/or are viewed as a substitute for participation in a state-sponsored plan. In some cases the post-retirement adjustments are financed in whole or in part by the government, while in other cases they are the responsibility of the sponsor of the pension plan.

The challenge of producing a continuing, regular retirement income throughout a person's retirement years is the greatest in the case of retirement programs that follow the individual savings model. Individual savings plans produce a stock of financial assets at retirement that retirees must convert into the flow of income they will use to support themselves for the rest of their lives. In order to do this, they need a strategy for dealing with two major sources of uncertainty: uncertainty about how long they will live and uncertainty about the course of the economy over the rest of their lives. These are the two sources of uncertainty that are handled automatically in most publicly managed defined benefit pension plans. Also, to the extent that the financial assets were accumulated in a mandated retirement saving program, the government will want to be sure that the public purposes of the mandate are achieved by preventing retirees from drawing them down too rapidly and exhausting them prematurely.

This chapter discusses the nature of the uncertainty about how long retirees will live and what will happen to wage and price levels after they retire and explores the approaches that can be taken for dealing with these sources of uncertainty. All such approaches require the use of fairly sophisticated financial institutions and markets, and several work best if government continues to play an active role in the retirement income system. Where sophisticated financial markets do not exist, they will have to be created before individual savings plans can be an effective alternative to defined benefit pensions.

THE SOURCES OF UNCERTAINTY

Uncertain lifespan. Chart 1 shows the expected distribution of remaining life spans for a representative cohort of people entering retirement at age 65 in the year 2000.[1] In this cohort, 90 percent of the people can expect to live at least five years after retiring, half can expect to live at least 16 years in retirement, 10 percent can expect to survive for at least 28 years, and 5 percent will still be alive in 2030, 30 years after retiring.

When paying pensions to a large group of retirees, the number that can be expected to live to each age level can be predicted with a fair degree of certainty. Predicting how long a specific individual will live is far more difficult. The individual retiree needs to know, however, how to spend down a stock of assets in such a way that they do not run out prematurely. Knowing their parents' lifespans and their own health, some workers may have strong indications either that they can expect a relatively short retirement or that their assets are going to have to last a long time. Most workers, however, will not know for sure whether to plan on being in the 10 percent that die within five years or the 5 percent that live for more than 30 years. If they are to finance themselves throughout retirement from a stock of assets that they bring into their retirement years, they will need a strategy for dealing with this uncertainty.

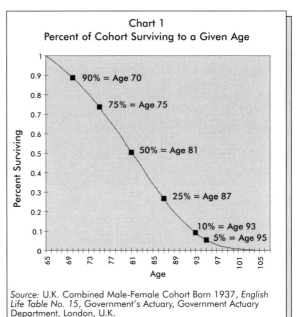

Chart 1
Percent of Cohort Surviving to a Given Age

90% = Age 70
75% = Age 75
50% = Age 81
25% = Age 87
10% = Age 93
5% = Age 95

Source: U.K. Combined Male-Female Cohort Born 1937, English Life Table No. 15, Government's Actuary, Government Actuary Department, London, U.K.

Under a government-mandated, individual savings plan, the government has a similar concern. The government may have mandated a minimum rate of contribution to an individual savings plan as a means either of offsetting worker myopia or of preventing excessive reliance on social safety net programs. In either case, the same logic that motivated the government to mandate contributions during working years also calls for restricting the pace at which assets can be withdrawn during retirement years.

Uncertain price and wage developments. A monthly income which appears quite adequate at the beginning of a retirement period can become inadequate if prices rise and the monthly income does not. Because retirement can last a long time, eventually even relatively modest rates of inflation

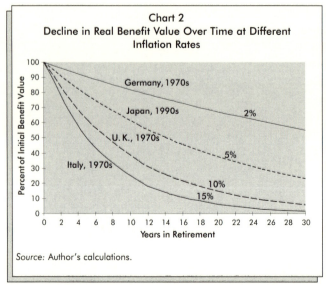

Chart 2
Decline in Real Benefit Value Over Time at Different Inflation Rates

Source: Author's calculations.

will seriously erode the purchasing power of a fixed monthly benefit.

Chart 2 traces how the purchasing power of a fixed benefit will decline over time at different rates of inflation. At a 15 percent rate of inflation (roughly the average experienced in Italy during the 1970s), half of the purchasing power is gone within five years. Sixteen years into retirement, when perhaps half of the cohort is still alive, the purchasing power would be just over 10 percent of its original value.

Even a relatively modest rate of inflation will cause serious erosion during the average retirement span in many OECD countries. At a 5 percent rate of inflation (roughly the rate experienced in Japan in the first half of the 1990s), a constant benefit will have lost half of its purchasing power within 14 years. And for those relatively few retirees who will still be alive 25 to 30 years after retirement, even a 2 percent annual inflation rate (normally equated with essentially stable prices), can take away 40 to 45 percent of the purchasing power of a benefit.

Because of the power of compounding of even modest inflation rates over relatively long retirement periods, effective retirement income systems need to incorporate some mechanism for adjusting the purchasing power of retirement benefits, should subsequent economic developments make it both necessary and feasible.

DEALING WITH THE UNCERTAINTY OF INFLATION AFTER RETIREMENT

Pay-as-you-go pensions. In an adequately financed pay-as-you-go pension program, pension benefits can easily be adjusted periodically to reflect changes in the average wage level of contributors. No matter how sharp the wage changes might be, at a constant contribution rate they will automatically cause pension program receipts to change by the same percentage amount as the wages changed, thereby allowing an equal, simultaneous change in pension benefits. A number of OECD countries use an index of average earnings to adjust benefits in their public pension programs, thereby ensuring that benefit changes also reflect trends in living standards among the working-age population.

Under normal economic conditions, pay-as-you-go pension plans are able to adjust pension amounts for changes in prices as easily as they could for changes in wages, since wage levels tend, over time, to adjust to reflect changes in price levels. The wage-price relationship does not necessarily hold in every year, though, and can be upset for an extended period of time during major economic upheaval. Wage adjustments can fall behind price changes—real wages can fall—when external events cause sharp price changes (such as the oil shocks of the 1970s) or when major economic transitions disrupt the productive process (as occurred in the states of the former Soviet Union during the early 1990s).

Real wage declines mean that workers' earnings are not keeping up with inflation. Retirement benefits will suffer the same fate if they are indexed to earnings. Where benefits have been indexed to prices, however, the retirees will initially be protected from a fall in living standards.

In these circumstances, the extent and timing of updates in retirement benefits will have to take into account assessments of the causes of the real wage decline. In the case of a temporary price spike, the public policy decision may be to maintain the real value of pension benefits for several years to see if real wage levels recover fairly quickly. In such a case, contribution income will not immediately rise by enough to fully finance the pension adjustment, and extra funds will have to come either from the government budget or from the reserves of the system (if sufficient). Alternatively, and particularly if the decline in real wages is likely to be prolonged, public policy may allow the real value of retirement benefits to decline in line with the decline in real wages.

Advance funded, defined benefit pensions. In defined benefit plans, initial pension levels are specified in relationship to the level of the retiree's previous earnings, frequently with a particularly heavy weight on earnings just prior to retirement. In developing the plans for funding these pensions, their sponsors must make projections about the pace at which earnings will rise in the future, schedule their advance payments in anticipation of future earnings growth, and develop procedures for adjusting the funding plans if their earnings projections turn out to be wrong. In principle, this same process can be used to finance adjustments to the benefits of those already retired, should the plan sponsor decide to offer such adjustments.[2]

Individual accounts. Adjustments in the amounts drawn out of individual accounts depend on strategies that involve the use of financial markets. In well-functioning financial markets the interest rate set by the market represents the prevailing real interest rate plus the market's assessment of the expected future inflation rate.

If inflation rates were as regular and predictable as the examples in chart 2, financial markets would immediately adjust interest rates to reflect them. Individuals entering retirement could then organize their financial affairs to offset the effects of future inflation. This can be done quite easily by basing all financial decisions on the real (i.e., inflation-adjusted) interest rate. By reinvesting each year that portion of the interest earnings that represents the inflation premium, the individual would be in a position each year to increase the amount being drawn down at a rate that would just offset the impact of inflation.

The problem, of course, is that inflation rates are not regular and predictable, with the result that the inflation premium which market forces have built into the interest rate may turn out to be either too high or too low. Thus, a retiree relying on market interest rates to provide inflation protection may experience windfall gains or be exposed to unexpected losses.

Chart 3 suggests the magnitude of these windfall gains and unexpected losses over the last couple of decades in four OECD countries. The chart shows how accurately the financial markets in these countries predicted medium-term inflation rates, by comparing the prediction of the cumulative 10-year inflation rate that was imbedded in each country's 10-year government bond rate to the actual inflation over that 10-year period.[3]

Over the years shown in chart 3, financial markets were not particularly adept at predicting 10-year average inflation rates. From the mid-1960s through the mid-1970s, many of the retirees relying on these market predictions would have ended up losing some 20 to 30 percent of their accumulated wealth to inflation not anticipated by the market. Losses would have been the smallest in Germany (averaging about 14 percent from 1966 through 1973) and the largest in the U.K. (averaging about 76 percent from 1966 through 1973).

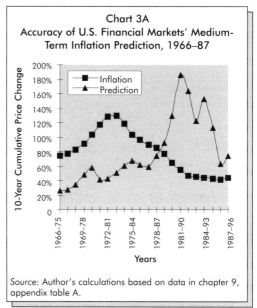

Chart 3A
Accuracy of U.S. Financial Markets' Medium-Term Inflation Prediction, 1966–87

Source: Author's calculations based on data in chapter 9, appendix table A.

In contrast to the unexpected losses in the earlier years of the period, retirees investing in the first half of the 1980s would have experienced large windfall gains when the markets' assessment of future inflation turned out to be far too high. Once again, inflation rates were more predictable (and windfall gains smaller) in Germany than in the other three countries. Among German retirees, the biggest winners would have been those who purchased 10-year bonds in 1981

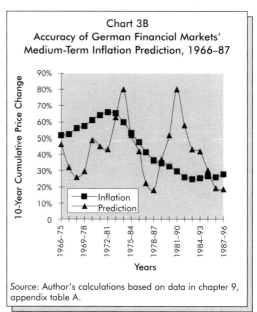

Chart 3B
Accuracy of German Financial Markets' Medium-Term Inflation Prediction, 1966–87

Source: Author's calculations based on data in chapter 9, appendix table A.

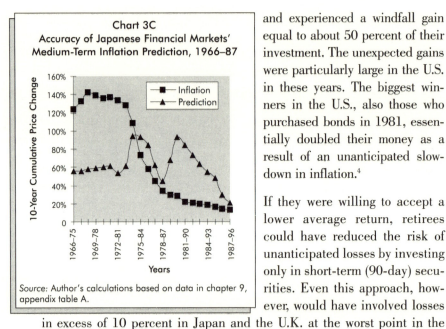

Chart 3C
Accuracy of Japanese Financial Markets' Medium-Term Inflation Prediction, 1966–87

Source: Author's calculations based on data in chapter 9, appendix table A.

and experienced a windfall gain equal to about 50 percent of their investment. The unexpected gains were particularly large in the U.S. in these years. The biggest winners in the U.S., also those who purchased bonds in 1981, essentially doubled their money as a result of an unanticipated slowdown in inflation.[4]

If they were willing to accept a lower average return, retirees could have reduced the risk of unanticipated losses by investing only in short-term (90-day) securities. Even this approach, however, would have involved losses in excess of 10 percent in Japan and the U.K. at the worst point in the 1970s' oil spike, and involved cumulative losses of 20 to 25 percent of the value of the portfolio in at least three of the countries during the 1970s. The strategy would have yielded windfall gains of 4 to 6 percent per year in several years in the mid-1980s.

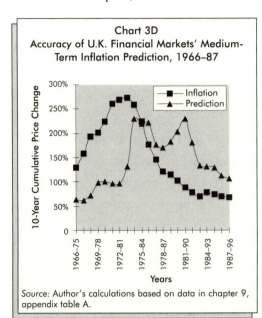

Chart 3D
Accuracy of U.K. Financial Markets' Medium-Term Inflation Prediction, 1966–87

Source: Author's calculations based on data in chapter 9, appendix table A.

Over the last couple of decades, governments in several countries have begun issuing bonds whose principal and interest are explicitly indexed to a measure of domestic consumer prices.[5] These bonds provide both retirees and those saving for retirement with an instrument that guarantees a real return no matter what might happen to future inflation rates. In effect, the government assumes all of the risk associated with unanticipated inflation. This allows individuals to make their retirement plans on the basis of an assured real rate of return, without having to worry about unanticipated losses (or having the chance to experience windfall gains). Indexed bonds in the U.K. have yielded a real return of between 3.5 and 5.0 percent, those in Chile have averaged 6.7 percent, and those in Canada yield about 4.5 percent. The first issue of such bonds in the U.S. guarantees a 3.4 percent real return.

If a government is willing to issue index bonds, it can organize a retirement income system based on mandatory, advance funded, individual accounts that is just as effective as a pay-as-you-go public pension system in protecting individual retirees from the risk of unanticipated inflation. Use of indexed bonds to achieve this result, however, has two important implications: a substantial portion of the financial assets held in individual retirement programs would have to be government liabilities, and the government would be guaranteeing the purchasing power of retiree assets in all economic circumstances to an even greater degree than it does under pay-as-you-go pension arrangements.

Public pay-as-you-go pension systems are sometimes criticized because they create implicit promises of future government payments and pass the responsibility for fulfilling these promises on to future taxpayers. Indexed bonds have the same characteristics. Using them to ensure adequate inflation protection in a retirement income system that is built around individual accounts reintroduces a pay-as-you-go element into the system and creates a floor below which the volume of the public sector debt cannot fall. Even if the use of such bonds were restricted to the accounts of those who had already retired, the aggregate amount outstanding at any given time might easily be as much as one-third of the total liabilities of the retirement income system.[6]

The commitment to index a bond, particularly one which trades on the open market, is likely to be more difficult to alter than is the commitment to index retirement benefits in a pay-as-you-go pension system. In the event of serious and prolonged economic distress, retirees under a system relying on individual accounts and indexed bonds may actually be better protected from inflation than those under an indexed, pay-as-you-go system. In contrast, a government that has issued large amounts of indexed bonds is likely to find that the existence of these bonds compounds its fiscal problems at such times.

Dealing with the Uncertainty of Individual Lifespans

Defined benefit pensions. Most defined benefit pension programs—whether privately or publicly managed, advance funded or pay-as-you-go—provide benefits in the form of monthly payments which continue for the life of the recipient. In principle, these plans could, but generally do not, allow retiring workers the option of taking some or all of their pension as a lump sum.

The advantage of lifetime payments is that all workers are guaranteed that their monthly income will continue for as long as they live, thereby protecting their economic status and minimizing social safety net expenditures. Making good on this guarantee requires a system for transferring the economic resources that would otherwise have been used to support those who die early to support those who live a long time.

It is this system of transfers that also accounts for the major disadvantage of life annuities. Under a system of life annuities, people who expect that they will not live as long as the cohort's average life expectancy are prevented from drawing a higher monthly benefit in the few years remaining or in using the extra resources as a bequest to their heirs.[7] For this reason, when retiring workers are offered annuities as an option, those who elect to take the annuity tend to live longer than those who do not. (In the language of insurance markets, sellers of individual annuities experience "adverse selection.")

Individual accounts. Those who plan on financing their retirement from their accumulated savings need a strategy to judge the pace at which these savings can be drawn down without running too great a risk of outliving their assets. Governments also need a strategy to ensure that retirement accounts are not drawn down too quickly. Several approaches are possible; each has its own advantages and disadvantages.

Live off of the interest. The simplest and surest way to avoid outliving one's assets is to never spend them. Retirees following this strategy would spend an amount each year equal to the real interest rate being earned on their portfolio, reinvesting the balance to allow their portfolio to grow by enough to offset any inflation in the economy. Subject to the kind of risks from unanticipated inflation discussed earlier, this strategy will allow a continued stream of income to even those who live the longest.

The advantages of this approach are the assurance that retirees will not outlive their assets and the ability of retirees to leave large bequests to their heirs, since their asset accumulations will never be drawn down. The disadvantage, of course, is that a rather substantial amount of assets has to be accumulated in order to generate even a modest retirement income, as is shown in table 1. The volume of assets necessary to pursue this strategy is simply the desired annual income divided by the average real rate of return that can be earned. At real interest rates prevailing on longer-term government bonds over the last four decades, retirees in the U.K. would have to accumulate assets equal to some 55 times their annual target retirement income, those in Japan and the U.S. would need at least 40 times their target, and German retirees would have to have some 25 times their target income. If they were willing to hold half of their assets in equities, the necessary accumulations are about 25 times the target.[8]

Employ a rule of thumb. Financial advisors have developed rules of thumb about the speed at which a portfolio can be drawn down based on historical market patterns. The rule will depend on the financial history of the particular country (and the assumption that the future will mirror the past), the composition of the investment portfolio, the length of time that one expects to live (and hence over which the assets must extend), and the risk one is willing to assume that the rule might fail.

One recent study based on an analysis of 70 years of U.S. financial history concluded that retirees could draw down 4 percent of their assets each year with only minimal risk of their portfolio not lasting at least 30 years; those drawing down 5 percent per year ran one chance in five of running out of assets in less than 30 years.[9] Under this rule of thumb, each year's drawdown is increased over the previous year's to reflect price changes. Retirees wishing to employ the 4 percent rule of thumb would have to accumulate assets equal to 25 times their target annual retirement income; those willing to use a 5 percent rule of thumb would need 20 times their target annual income in retirement. These are also rather ambitious goals for a retirement saving program.

Programmed withdrawals. In their system of privately managed individual accounts, the Chileans address the uncertainty of lifespan in two ways. Worker risk is minimized by their ability (at their option) to purchase indexed life annuities. If they choose not to purchase such annuities, they may draw down the balance in their accounts. In this case, however, the government's interest in preventing overuse of the safety net is protected by a particular rule of thumb which limits the speed at which assets can be withdrawn from the individual accounts. The approach involves calculating the maximum permissible annual payment each year for each retiree based on the balance in the retiree's account, the retiree's current life expectancy, and an average real rate of return set annually by the regulatory authorities.

The Chilean rule is not intended to provide the same assurance that assets will be sufficient throughout retirement that an annuity would provide. For this reason, it allows substantially larger annual drawdowns than do the rules discussed previously, and drawing down at this pace implies the need for substantially less accumulation as a worker enters retirement. Simulations suggest that an average worker in Chile who drew the maximum amount allowed by the rule each year would find the annual draw to be smaller each year than it had been the previous year until, after about 15 years, it fell below the minimum pension level guaranteed by the Chilean state.[10]

Annuities. In principle, workers can use the assets accumulated in their individual accounts to purchase life annuities, thereby producing the same kind of lifetime retirement income stream that is supplied by defined benefit occupational and pay-as-you-go public pension systems. As shown in table 1, ignoring administrative costs and assuming that annuities are priced using the mortality experience of the whole cohort, males retiring in Japan, Germany, the U.K., and the U.S. could buy life annuities indexed to the inflation rate for between 9 and 13 times the desired annual benefit. Joint and survivor annuities that guaranteed 75 percent of the annual benefit to a surviving spouse would cost about 15 to 25 percent more. (Country differences reflect differences in life expectancy and in prevailing real interest rates.)

The individual annuity option may not be quite as attractive in practice as it appears in these numbers, however. For one thing, individual annuities cannot be purchased at the prices implied here in most countries because, among other things, of the problem of adverse selection. Indeed, the problem of adverse selection in individual annuity markets is one of the reasons that has been advanced to justify government intervention in the retirement income system.[11] Annuity returns available in the private market are also lower than the figures shown in table 1, owing to the impact of administrative and sales expenses and the profits that the annuity issuers must earn in order to offer reasonable returns to shareholders.

One analysis of the market for individual annuities in the United States found that actual annuity prices for 65-year-old men in 1995 averaged some 22 percent higher than would be expected based on prevailing mortality rates and assuming the alternative is to invest in government bonds.[12] The study found that adverse selection accounted for about 13 percent differential. The rest can be ascribed to expenses and profit. In Chile, the interest rates used in the computation of individual annuities were, on average, 2.08 percentage points lower than those prevailing on comparable long-term government bonds. An interest rate differential of this size would, by itself, raise the price of an annuity by about 17 percent.[13] The interest rate differential is one of the ways in which the Chilean insurance companies adjust for adverse selection.

Adverse selection problems are less severe if all participants in a mandatory savings program are forced to buy annuities. Until recently, the personal pension system in the U.K. had such a requirement. This requirement probably helps explain why the mortality experience for purchasers of annuities in the U.K. is much closer to that for the population as a whole than it is in the U.S.[14]

A second problem confronting the purchaser of an individual annuity involves adjustments in the periodic payments to reflect changes in wage and price levels. Standard annuities are long-term contracts with fixed payments whose real value will decline if price levels rise over time. Such benefit erosion can be prevented by purchasing a variable annuity, which is an annuity whose payments are adjusted periodically to reflect changes in the value of a particular portfolio of investments. In particular, where a variable annuity based on a portfolio of price-indexed bonds is available, it will provide lifetime inflation protection. Price-indexed annuities of this sort are required if the annuity option is selected in the Chilean system.

A third challenge concerns the timing of the purchase of an annuity.[15] Once an annuity is purchased, the terms and conditions determining the value of its periodic payments are locked in. Those who reach retirement age in a year in which the value of their portfolios is temporarily depressed will find that an annuity purchased at that time permanently reduces their retirement income. In contrast, those who reach retirement age in a year in which investments are doing unusually well will have a permanent advantage when they purchase their annuity.

These fluctuations in the value of underlying retirement portfolios—and their implications for lifetime retirement incomes—provide one of the major arguments against mandating the purchase of annuities. Absent a mandate, retiring workers will not find themselves forced to annuitize a portfolio whose value is temporarily depressed, but the price they pay may be that all annuities are somewhat more expensive due to the risk of adverse selection to the annuity provider.

A final major difference between the group approaches common in defined benefit pension plans and the individual approaches common in retirement savings programs concerns the impact of gender on life expectancy. Group plans tend to pay the same monthly benefit to similarly situated persons regardless of gender. Individual annuities are almost always sold on a gender-specific basis, with women (who can be expected to live longer) receiving lower annual payments than similarly situated men. In principle, gender-specific calculations could be prohibited in private annuities, although enforcing such a provision might prove difficult.

SUMMARY

Planning for retirement requires dealing with two major sources of uncertainty, unexpected inflation and uncertain lifespans. Traditional pay-as-you-go public pension programs deal with these problems by paying benefits in the form of life annuities adjusted to reflect current economic conditions. Private pension programs that are advance funded and operate on the defined benefit basis also commonly pay lifetime benefits. In the absence of some form of government subsidy, however, it is less common for these programs to guarantee that their pensions will be adjusted once payments have begun.

Those seeking to live through retirement by drawing down financial assets need to find alternative strategies. Governments that have used a mandatory individual savings approach to ensure that workers make adequate provision for retirement face the related challenge of ensuring that newly retired workers do not draw down their assets too quickly.

Well-developed private financial markets are capable of offering approaches that reduce both forms of uncertainty. In even the most sophisticated financial markets, however, the strategies available suffer from serious limitations in the absence of some form of government intervention. The strategies become much more effective if government is willing to assume the responsibility of issuing bonds indexed to reflect changes in retail prices and to mandate that retirees convert all or a part of their accumulated assets into annuities.

Both of these potential government actions have disadvantages, however. The disadvantage of issuing indexed bonds is that they create a pay-as-you-go liability which, though likely to be smaller than that associated with a pay-as-you-go public pension system, is actually less amenable to modification in times of economic distress. In addition to possible philosophical objections, the disadvantage to mandating the purchase of annuities is that it may permanently harm cohorts who happen to reach retirement age at a time when the value of investment portfolios is temporarily depressed.

Notes

1. This happens to be a combined male-female life table for the cohort born in the U.K. in 1937.

2. The financial adjustments triggered by unanticipated increases in the benefits of those already retired are somewhat more challenging than those for unanticipated increases in the initial benefits of those who will be retiring in the future, however, since the liabilities for the former come due immediately whereas the extra liability associated with the latter can be paid off over time.

3. For the purposes of charts 3A–D, the market's prediction is derived by subtracting from the nominal interest rate actually paid on the bond the long-term average real interest rate that prevailed on 10-year bonds in each country over the 10-year holding periods 1966–75 through 1987–96. The average real interest rates that were deducted were 4.0 percent in Germany, 2.2 percent in Japan, 2.5 percent in the U.S., and 1.8 percent in the U.K.

4. The unanticipated gains experienced by purchasers of these government bonds were matched by unanticipated losses experienced the sellers of the bonds, which provides part of the explanation for the persistent budget deficits in the mid-1980s, particularly in the U.S.

5. Indexed bonds were issued for the first time in an OECD country in the U.K. in 1981 and have since grown to represent 18 percent of total outstanding government debt in the U.K. Similar indexed bonds have been issued by the governments of Sweden, Canada, Israel, Chile, and the U.S., among others. Outside of several Latin American countries, private sector organizations have generally not issued indexed bonds.

6. The relationship between potential account balances and average wages was discussed in the earlier chapter on choices of pension approaches and transitions between approaches.

7. Annuity providers often offer an option in which a certain number of payments are guaranteed no matter how soon an individual dies. Uncertainty works both ways. These guarantees, which typically run for 5 or 10 years, serve to diminish the risk of loss should an annuity purchaser die after only one payment.

8. Assumes that portfolios are divided equally between medium-term government bonds and equities, and earn real returns at the average historical rate over the period 1953–95.

9. The author found that drawing down at a rate of 5 percent per year would have caused 11 cohorts (of 50 simulated) to exhaust their assets before 30 years; five of them exhausted their assets in around 20 years. These results apply to portfolios that were half stocks and half treasury bills, though changes in portfolio composition turn out to have little impact on the results. See William P. Bengen, "Determining Withdrawal Rates Using Historical Data," *Journal of Financial Planning* 7:4 (October 1994), 171–80.

10. Diaz, C.A., "Analisis Crítico de las Modalidades de Pensión y Propuesta Alternativa," Working Paper 156 (Santiago, Chile: Instituto de Economía, Pontificia Universidad Católica de Chile).

11. See the chapter on reasons for creating mandatory retirement programs.

12. Mitchell, Olivia S., James M. Poterba, and Mark J. Warshawsky, "New Evidence on the Money's Worth of Individual Annuities," Working Paper No. 6002 (Cambridge, Mass.: National Bureau of Economic Research, April 1997). This is an update of the analysis first presented in Mark Warshawsky, "Private Annuity Markets in the United States: 1919–1984," *Journal of Risk and Insurance* (1988).

13. Interest rates are from Peter Diamond and Salvador Valdes-Prieto, "Social Security Reforms," ed. Barry P. Bosworth, Rudiger Dornbusch, and Raul Laban, *The Chilean Economy: Policy Lessons and Challenges*, 257–319. The life table used was the U.S. life table for a male born in 1935, *Life Tables for the U.S. Social Security Area, 1900–2080*, Actuarial Study No. 107 (Department of Health and Human Services, Social Security Administration, Office of the Actuary, August 1992).

14. The observation about mortality tables in the U.K. comes from a comparison of the life table for the entire population of England and Wales based on 1990–92 deaths

(ELT No. 15) with the standard table for pensioners in insured pension schemes produced by the Continuous Mortality Investigation Bureau of the Faculty and Institute of Actuaries for persons attaining age 60 in 1997. Holders of personal pensions are required to annuitize at least 75 percent of their assets, but beginning in 1996 can postpone doing so until they reach age 75.

15. This issue is explained more fully in the chapter on risks of mid-career economic and demographic change.

APPENDIX TABLE A
Assets Required under Different Retirement Income Strategies
(Ratio of assets at retirement to initial retirement income)
Assumes incomes adjusted for inflation after retirement

Strategy	Germany	Japan	U.K.	U.S.
Live Off the Interest				
Government Bonds	25.8	45.5	55.5	40.0
Bond/Equity Mix	26.7	22.4	23.2	23.5
Rule of Thumb				
4% Drawdown	25.0	25.0	25.0	25.0
5% Drawdown	20.0	20.0	20.0	20.0
Pure Annuity				
65-Year-Old Male	10.8	9.6	8.0	11.0
65-Year-Old Female	12.7	15.6	15.4	12.8
Assumptions				
Inflation (%)	3.5	4.7	8.2	6.1
Average Real Bond Returns (%)	4.0	2.2	1.8	2.5
Average Real Equity Returns (%)	3.5	6.7	6.8	6.0
Life Expectancy at 65				
Males	13.8	16.7	13.6	16.3
Females	17.6	19.7	19.6	20.6

Notes: The government bond rate is the average rate of interest on 10-year government securities over the period 1965–95. Sources for government bond rates and inflation data are listed in chapter 9, appendix table A.

The bond/equity mix assumes portfolios are held 50 percent in 10-year government bonds and 50 percent in a broad mix of equities whose performance matches that of the respective country's entire equity market. Source for equity returns are listed in chapter 9, appendix table A.

Pure annuity numbers reflect the expected value of a single-life annuity purchased at age 65 assuming interest at the 10-year government bond rate and gender-specific mortality that reflects the experience of the population as a whole. The actual price of an annuity could be anywhere from 15 to 25 percent higher to reflect sales and operating expenses, profit, taxes, and the impact of adverse selection.

Source: Annuity calculations use the real interest rates and life expectancies shown in the table. Life tables used were for the U.S. cohort born in 1935 as reported in *Life tables for the United States Social Security Area, 1900-2080*, Actuarial Study No. 107 (Office of the Actuary, Social Security Administration, August 1992); for the U.K. cohort born in 1937 as reported in *English Life Table No. 15* (Government's Actuary, Government Actuary Department, London, England, 1997); and mortality rates for the Japanese population in 1990 as reported in the *17th Life table* (Government of Japan), and in Bruce D. Schobel and Robert J. Myers, "A Century of Japanese Mortality Experience," 1993–94 Transactions of the Society of Actuaries Reports. Life expectancy is life expectancy at age 65 for most recent year available as reported in *Averting the Old Age Crisis* (World Bank, 1994), table A.10, 371–2.

Index

A

administrative costs, 14–15, 104–108, 110, 112n.14
advance funded systems, 20, 98, 146n.3
   approaches to, 57–58
   contribution rates, 133
   financial markets and, 66, 69n.22
   fiscal challenges of, 124–127
   inflation and, 156
   savings and, 8–9, 66–67
   shift to from pay-as-you-go plans, 43–44
   studies of, 60–61
age dependency ratio, 42, 48n.10
age of worker, work effort and, 9–10, 73–74
aggregate consumption ratio, 6–7, 40–41, 42, 47, 49
aging population, 7, 20, 41–42
   costs of, 121
   pension programs and, 27
   standard of living and, 29
annuities, 31–32, 134, 146n.9, 160, 162–164, 166n.7
   cost of, 15, 106
   indexed, 36n.4
   variable, 19
Argentina, pension liabilities, 127
asset accumulation patterns, 57–58
asset exchanges, 38, 39, 47n.4
asset holdings, 138–141, 146n.8, 160–164

B

banking, pension plans and, 65–66
birth rate, 100–104, 142–143
bonds, 19, 140–141, 158, 166n.4
Brittain, John A., 94n.2

C

Canada
   debt/GDP ratio, 128, 129
   pension liabilities, 131n.9
   savings and, 60
capital income, 38
capital markets, 44, 67n.1
capital ownership, 47n.2
capital stock, 65
capitalization retirement systems, 39
Chand, Sheetal K., 128
Chile
   annuities, 163
   labor markets, 82n.6
   pension liabilities, 127
   pension plans, 74n.2, 162
   recognition bonds, 131n.8
Cifuentes, Rodrigo, 65
competitiveness, international
   labor costs and, 91–92
   overview, 85–86
   social security systems and, 11–12, 20–21, 86–88, 96
   statistical relationships, 92–93, 96
compliance, costs of, 27
compulsory participation in plans, 32–33
consumption, 6–7, 37–40, 46, 67n.2, 67n.3
   lifecycle theory of, 54
   measure of, 47n.5
   reduction in, 53
   taxes, 69n.19
contribution rates, 46, 97
   advance funded systems, 133
   birthrate and, 100–104
   demographics and, 13, 100–104, 113
   factors dependent upon, 14, 100–104

free market economy and, 88–90
funded, defined benefit pension systems and, 13–14, 98
individual accounts, 149
individual savings plans and, 13–14, 97–98, 102–103
interest rates and, 111n.7
life expectancies and, 13–14, 131n.4
mandatory contributions, 56
misestimates impact, 134–135
model for, 137
pay-as-you-go systems, 48n.12, 103–104, 109–110, 143, 146n.2
set-aside amount, 17
take-home pay relationship, 11
wages and, 101, 104
worker behavior and, 9, 72–73
contributions/benefits link, 12–14, 21, 29, 48n.12, 56–57, 97–98, 118, 121–122
compliance incentives and, 76–77
Germany, 144
pension promises and, 17–18, 144–145
private sector and, 74
rate estimate mismatches, 134–135
strengthening of, 10–11, 73–76
contributor/pensioner ratio, 13–1419
contributory pensions, 39

D

Dean, Andrew, 62–63
debt, 16, 125–127, 128–129
defined benefit pension systems, 31, 36n.3
approaches to, 117–118
birthrate and, 101
changing conditions and, 18
contribution rates under, 12–14, 97–98
life expectancies and, 160
objectives of, 15–16, 115–116
risk of, 18
demographics
contribution rates and, 13, 100–104, 113
pension entitlements and, 135–137, 141–144

rate of return and, 15
retirement benefits effects and, 141–142
shifts in, 7, 41–42
trends in, 47n.3
Diamond, Peter A., 36n.1
dollar, U.S., 91–92
Durand, Martine, 62–63

E

earnings levels, 30, 31
economic growth
OECD, 134
retirement income and, 30, 31
savings and, 52–54
economic issues
aggregate consumption ratio, 6–7, 40–41, 42, 47
approaches to, 5–6
financial markets and, 65–66
international trade and, 11–12, 86–88
living standards ratio, 6–7, 40–41, 42, 47
long-term trends, 137–140
measure of, 5
pension entitlements and, 135–141
pension plans and, 18
retiree dependency ratio, 6–7, 40–41, 42, 47
retiree support, 37–40
retirees' risks and, 19
retirement income, 28
savings and, 54
views of pension plans and labor supply, 72–76
see also economic growth
employees
pension contributions and, 88–90
pensions costs, 20–21
employer costs, 20–21
employment taxes, 77
equities, investment, 140–141
equity returns, 140–141, 146n.6
European Monetary Union, 92
European Union, 92
exchange rates and, 12, 91–92, 93, 124

exchange rates, labor costs and, 12,
    91–92, 93

F

Fallon, John, 62–63
Feldstein, Martin, 36n.1, 65
financial markets, 65–66, 158–159
foreign capital, 67n.1
France, pension liabilities, 125–126
free market economy, pension
    contributions and, 88–90
funded, defined benefit pension
    systems, contribution rates and,
    13–14, 98

G

GDP *see* gross domestic product (GDP)
Germany
    annuities, 162
    birth rate, 143
    contribution/benefit link, 144
    debt/GDP ratio, 128, 129
    economic data, 148
    equity returns, 140–141
    inflation, 157–158
    pension contribution rate, 137–139
    pension entitlements, 135–137
    pension liabilities, 125–126
    savings and, 60
goods and services, 37–40
government interventions, retirement
    programs, 3–5, 26–27
    arguments for, 3–5
    income redistribution and, 4,
        29–30, 35
    myopic view of, 3–4, 28, 32–34,
        35
    protection of prudent society
        members, 4, 29
    rationale for, 35
    responses to, 32
    structure of, 32–34
government policies, social security
    contributions and, 11–12
government-mandated, individual
    savings plans, 153
gross domestic product (GDP), 12, 93,
    96

costs and, 23n.1
debt/GDP ratio, 128
pension liabilities and, 125–127
savings/pension relationship,
    62–64
social security as percent of, 96
gross national savings, pension assets
    and, 62–64
Gruber, Jonathan, 94n.2

H

health status, 78
Hoeller, Peter, 62–63
Holmlund, Bertil, 95n.5
home mortgage loans, 81n.3
Hungary, pension reforms, 65

I

immigration policies, 48n.10
imprudent society members, 4, 29,
    33–34, 35
income
    effect on retirement, 45
    take-home pay, 11, 75, 89
    taxes and, 78
    worker behavior and, 9, 73, 81n.2
income redistribution, 4, 29–30, 35
indexed bonds, 19, 32, 159, 166n.5
individual accounts, 159–164
individual savings systems, 101
    approaches to, 117–118
    contribution rates and, 13–14,
        97–98, 102–103, 113
    retirement income and, 152
industrial countries, pension plan
    liabilities, 125–127, 128–129
inflation, 18–19, 30, 31, 34–35, 154
    benefits and, 152–153
    retirement uncertainties and,
        155–159
interest rates
    contribution rate and, 14,
        101–104, 111n.7, 113
    retirement benefits and, 160–161
    wage rate relationship, 135–139

International Institute for Management Development, Lausanne, Switzerland, 87, 93
International Social Security Association (ISSA), 1–3
international trade *see* competitiveness, international
interventions *see* government interventions, retirement programs
intrafamily pension systems, 58, 68n.9
investment portfolio, 161, 162, 166n.8, 166n.9
investments, 52, 67n.1
   see also savings
Italy, debt/GDP ratio, 128, 129

J

Jaeger, Albert, 128
Japan
   annuities, 162
   birth rate, 143
   contribution/benefit link, 144
   economic data, 148
   equity returns, 140–141
   inflation, 154
   life expectancy, 142
   pension contribution rate, 137–139
   pension entitlements, 135–137
   savings and, 60

K

Kotlikoff, Laurence J., 65

L

labor costs
   exchange rates and, 12, 91–92, 93
   international trade and, 91–92
   pension contributions and, 88–90
labor market, 10
labor supply
   pension plan transitions and, 124
   pension systems and, 9–11, 71–83
   policy implications for pensions on, 79–81
   social security impact on, 21
   studies of, 10, 77–79, 82n.7

Latin America
   pension reforms, 131n.7
   retirement plans, 43–44
life expectancies, 18–19, 30, 31–32, 48n.9, 80, 142, 145
   contribution rates and, 13–14, 131n.4
   gender and, 164
   impact on pension plans, 108–109
   impact of savings on, 34
   increase in, 41, 46
   lifetime payments and, 160
   pension benefits and, 160
lifecycle theory of consumption, 54
living standards ratio, 6–7, 40–41, 42, 46, 47, 49
longevity *see* life expectancies

M

mandatory pension systems, 38–39
   labor supply and, 21
   negative features of, 9
   objectives of, 71–72, 81n.1
   retirement age and, 10, 77, 78–79
mark, German, 91–92
market outcomes
   failure causes, 27–32
   government intervention in, 26–27
   retirement programs and, 33–34
market-generated income distribution, 29–30
maturation of plans, 16
mid-career workers, pension plans and, 124
monetary policies, 90
mortality rates, 48n.9
   annuities and, 162–164
   effects on pension plans, 14–15, 104–108, 111n.10, 113
   pay-as-you-go systems and, 142
   pension benefits and, 17, 135, 144–142
   preretirement, 112n.15
   trends, 30, 31, 135
multi-pillar systems, 16, 130
multiple-generation households, 38

N

national pension systems, 55–56, 58, 67n.4
national saving, 52–53
noncontributory systems, 15–16, 39
notional defined contribution plan, 110n.1, 123, 130n.1, 146n.3, 147n.11

O

occupational pension plans, 98
Organization for Economic Cooperation and Development (OECD)
  average earnings index, 155
  competitiveness rank, 12, 93, 96
  economic data, 148
  economic growth, 124
  funded plans and, 14, 104, 106
  pension liabilities of, 125–127
  pension/savings link, 8–9, 62–64
  population growth rates, 136–137
  inflation rates, 154, 156–157, 165n.3

P

pay-as-you-go systems
  adjustments to, 41–43
  approaches to, 57–58, 117, 131n.3, 134
  birthrate and, 100–104
  contribution rate model, 103–104, 111n.7
  contribution rates under, 12–14, 48n.12, 97–98, 109–110, 143, 146n.2
  criticisms of, 2
  fiscal problems of, 22
  inflation and, 155–159
  mortality and, 113, 142
  population growth and, 143
  risks of, 18, 19
  savings and, 8–9, 66–67, 113
  shift from to advance funding, 43–44
  transition to privately managed plan, 16–17, 119–120, 122–124

payroll tax, 95n.5
pension systems
  adjustments to, 156, 165n.2
  administrative costs, 14–15, 105–108, 110, 112n.14
  approaches to, 15–18, 45–46, 115–132
  compliance with, 4, 76–77
  contribution rates, 97
  costs, 5–7, 23n.1, 43–44
  creation of, 26
  debate review, 1–3
  finance of, 127–129
  financial issues of, 20–22
  form of benefits, 151
  GDP relationship, 125–127
  government intervention in, 3–5, 26–27
  labor supply and, 9–11, 71–83
  liabilities of, 125–127, 128–129
  management approach to, 74, 76
  mandatory contribution increases, 56
  maturation of, 16, 117
  model, 98–100, 103–104, 106–108, 110n.3
  myopic view of, 75
  national pension system, 55–56, 58, 67n.4
  objectives of, 15–16, 116–117
  participant behavior in, 4–5
  relationship to savings, 8–9, 51–52, 53–54
  risks of, 145–146
  role of, 2
  spending on as percent of GDP, 96
  studies of effect on savings, 9, 59–61, 66
  transition types, 15–18
  see also specific type of system
Pigou, A. C., 36n.1, 68n.9
politics, contribution/benefit link and, 121
population growth rates, 23n.3, 135–137, 143, 145
preretirement earnings, 17, 138–139
preretirement mortality, 112n.15
price index, 151
private insurance markets, 32

private pension systems
   benefits offered, 151–152
   Chile, 162
   retirement behavior and, 79, 82n.12
private sector
   costs of pension plans and, 42–43
   retirement plans and, 43–44, 46–47
privately managed systems, transition from pay-as-you-go plan, 16–17, 119–120, 122–124
pro-savings pension policies, 9
product prices, 89–90, 94n.4
provident fund model, 23n.4
public pension systems, 9, 23
   observations of, 4–5
   role of, 2–3
   structure of, 34
public policy
   pension plans, 120–122
   pensions and labor supply, 79–81
purchasing power, 38

R

recognition bonds, 124, 131n.8, 132n.10, 132n.11
relative burden, algebraic derivation of, 49
retired persons
   costs of support for, 40–41
   economic support for, 5–6, 37–40
   income strategies, 168
   inflation and, 155–159
   policies for support of, 7, 41–43, 46
   uncertainties of, 18–19, 152–154
retiree dependency ratio, 6–7, 40–42, 46, 47, 48n.10, 49
retirement, financing of, 47n.1, 48n.8
retirement age, 28
   health status and, 78, 79
   increase in, 42, 48n.11
   influence on, 10, 77, 78–79
   resources for, 34
retirement benefits, 23n.2, 78, 82n.11
retirement income, 21–22, 28

retirement insurance, provision problems, 30–31, 35
retirement programs, structure of, 32–34

S

savings
   consumption and, 54, 56, 67n.2, 67n.3
   economic gain of increases in, 65
   economic growth and, 52–54
   impact of retirement on, 34
   incentives for, 58
   national, 52–53
   OECD countries, 8–9, 62–64
   pay-as-you-go systems, 113
   pension systems and, 8–9, 51–52, 53–54, 67
   personal/national link, 62–64
   reductions in, 58
   studies of effect on pension plans, 9, 59–61, 66
Schmidt-Hebbel, Claus, 82n.6
self-employed, 10, 76, 80
Smetters, Kent, 65
social welfare, pension programs and, 26
standard of living, 7, 26, 28, 29, 34, 41–43, 45, 46
subsidies, 26, 29, 33, 75–76
supplemental retirement programs, 26
Sweden
   debt/GDP ratio, 128, 129
   pension liabilities, 131n.9
   savings and, 60

T

take-home pay, 11, 75, 89
tax compliance, 10, 11, 77–78
taxes
   employment, 77
   payroll, 95n.5
   pension programs and, 72–73
   worker behavior and, 77–78

U

unemployment, 12, 89, 90
unemployment insurance, 88
United Kingdom
  administrative costs of pension plans, 106
  annuities, 162, 163, 166n.14
  contribution/benefit link, 144
  economic data, 148
  equity returns, 140–141
  financial markets, 158–159
  pension contribution rate, 137–139
  pension entitlements, 135–137
  pension liabilities, 125–126
United States
  annuities, 162, 163
  contribution/benefit link, 144
  economic data, 148
  equity returns, 140–141
  inflation, 158–159
  life expectancy, 142
  pension contribution rate, 137–139
  pension entitlements, 135–137
  pension liabilities, 125–126
  pension plan administrative costs, 105–106
universal pension programs, 115, 117

V

Valdés-Prieto, Salvador, 65
value-added tax, 75–76

W

wage growth rate, 14, 102–104, 110n.6
wage rate/interest relationship, 135–139
wage-price relationship, 155
wages
  contribution rate and, 101, 104
  decline in, 155–156
  deductions from, 11, 89, 94n.4
  minimum, 90
  retirement benefits and, 110n.5
Walliser, Jan, 65
worker behavior, 9, 72–72, 80, 81n.2
workers, older, work effort and, 9–10, 73–74
working-age population, labor impacts on, 73
World Bank, 60

About the Author

Lawrence Thompson is a senior fellow at the Urban Institute in Washington, D.C. where he specializes in pension and retirement issues and serves as a consultant on pension reform to both the International Labor Office and the World Bank. He joined the Urban Institute after a 25-year career as both a policy analyst and social welfare program administrator in the U.S. government. His government career included serving as executive director of an Advisory Council on Social Security, director of Social Security Research and Statistics, and chief economist of the U.S. General Accounting Office. He also served as Assistant Comptroller General of the United States in charge of the review of social welfare programs and as the principal deputy commissioner and chief operating officer of the U.S. Social Security Administration. Mr. Thompson is currently the secretary and a member of the board of directors of the National Academy of Social Insurance and has previously been a member of the board of directors of the International Social Security Association. He holds a Ph.D. in economics from the University of Michigan and an M.B.A. from the Wharton School at the University of Pennsylvania, and is a graduate of Iowa State University.